VALLEY OF ANIMALS

Valley Of Animals

ELMA M. WILLIAMS

Illustrated

The John Day Company   New York

First American Edition 1966

Library of Congress Catalogue
Card Number: 66-11600

LOVE TO DIDI

LIST OF ILLUSTRATIONS

✳

A seat out of the sun

Family at work . . . and at play

Lissa's turn to make the tea

Then time for meditation

Beyond the oak woods, the estuary and the sea

Time off on Borth sands

Jane, with her whitest of white lambs

Llanarth Siriol, confidential cob

Au revoir

✳

The following photographs were taken by the author and John Hughes: illustration pages 5, 6 (upper), 7 (lower), 8 (both upper), 11, 14, 24 (lower), 25, 26, 28, 29, and 30.
All other photographs were taken by Helen Simpson of Woman's Mirror.

THE LORDLY ONES

They know the drift of days and nights, of moons and cool
    repose,
Of seasons stretching from hot sunshine to fire-lit hearths,
Even more of human passions than we could ever know:
Griefs that tear; devotion—cloying and the other sort—
Despair and deepest love. They are amused by these,
Some of them, and scratch their fleas or attend to graver
    sport.
In disorderly content they wander through the pages of our
    lives,
Spilling what they need upon themselves,
Discarding at leisure or pleasure the too absurd.
At a word or a cry one will lie down and die for its god.
Why? Ask the lordly ones; they know.
Their knowledge, their intimate *knowledge*, is a terrible thing.

Elma M. Williams

Chapter One

O<small>N</small> a cold, blustery night in February something croaked outside the kitchen door. Peering outside and shivering, it came as no surprise to see the ground already white and large snow-flakes beating against the yard light.

I knew that all my animals were safely indoors, and none fitted the croaking variety. I listened. The sound was not repeated, but in a shed, where my motor cycle was kept, an engine was running fitfully.

Novice to the art of motor cycling, I did know that such an engine does not tick over involuntarily. That particular engine knew no soft key; its gentlest sound was as a flight of jet planes. There was nothing else mechanical in the shed, but "Woo-oo, woo-oo!", it persisted.

So I knelt down and looked under the machine, prepared to find at least the petrol tap not turned off. My hand was stayed in its forward reach; my heart lurched uncomfortably.

I looked straight into the eyes of the Devil himself. He bade me go no nearer.

"Bell, book and candle!" I murmured, wriggling to an upright position and prepared to bolt to the house. Then reason took over. It was—it must be—a creature. Probably it was an owl.

Down again on the floor, I reached forward to grasp a feathery body and to draw it to safety. No feathery body was there; only a mass of wet fur and the curses of the damned. The hissing would have misled me still more, but I knew that snakes had neither wet fur nor great, luminous eyes. Between hisses and deep curses ran the non-stop woo-ooing. I put forward my hand again and the creature leapt into the yard, where I could see and understand.

That is inaccurate; I did not fully understand. I shall never do so. But, just then, I knew that I confronted the ugliest and most terrified cat I'd ever seen.

One eye was lower than the other. Its crooked ears were bent forward and the face was contorted, either by fear or pain.

"My poor sweet—come here!"

It darted aside and, unlike any cat I had known, stumbled. This was no time to take in the unusual symmetry of a stray cat. With such a wheezing chest, obviously it needed food and warmth. I went indoors, prepared a dish of meat and gravy, another of milk and took them outside.

There was no cat. I called, rattled the dishes and once thought I heard a wooing croak in the garden. Inspired, I took the dishes up the loft steps, leaving them on the platform and called: "Puss, it's here!"

No woo; no cat. I went indoors, wondering if I had imagined the misshapen animal.

When I realized that there were no paw marks across the yard I shivered with more than the cold. What I had seen, or thought I had seen, had been the embodiment of all—what? Evil, perhaps. Or was it *suffering*?

Familiar noses nudging me as I sat by the fire made me more reasonable. I laughed at my macabre thoughts, quickly arguing myself back to complete sanity. Naturally there had been no paw marks on my second visit to the yard. Snow was falling swiftly. A few minutes of such weather would obliterate even a human footprint.

So I forgot my strange visitor until early the next morning. I went to the loft and saw two empty dishes. Their contents had gone to some deserving cause. And, inside the loft, on drifted snow, were the imprints of a cat's paws.

The weather worsened. At the same time the next night I heard an ominous woo-oo outside. Nothing was to be seen but, again, I left food in the loft. For five nights I repeated that gesture to the anonymous, and each morning the dishes were empty. On the fifth morning I was rewarded by seeing my same waif crouching behind a bale of straw.

I was not allowed to touch him, although I tried. "Come on, Woo—come on, dear. I'm quite friendly, you know."

A ghastly sight was that fleeing cat. Its frenzied escape in the form of a crooked lope, because its forelegs were so much shorter than the hind, spoke ill of its opinion of mankind.

The weather improved. I found the dishes full on subsequent mornings. I soon forgot the crooked cat, whose end I could surmise more easily than its beginning. It would steal to live and, stealing, die.

A year passed swiftly, as years do when hard work is accompanied by a family of adoring animals.

Then it began to snow again, strangely, at the same time as the previous year. The dogs gave me a cooler morning greeting than usual. Their attention was focused on the kitchen door.

Three pekinese, two golden retrievers, a terrier and I stood, heads on one side, contemplating the sound of a muffled engine.

13

It—couldn't be. But, because the wooing and whirring reminded me of a crooked cat in the snow, I ordered: "Sit!" Two retrievers actually did sit. There was no urgent barking; just frank curiosity, which I shared.

Sure enough, I opened the door to a twisted, white figure. It uttered: "Woo-oo," scrambled forward on its stomach, past staring dogs, to the fire. There it collapsed in a heap. The white soon melted, giving way to dark tabby in an appalling state of disrepair.

The dogs were very good. They seemed to understand that something must be done, and quickly.

The first light touch of my hand on the emaciated body caused it to lurch forward a few steps, taking cover under the stove. Warm milk followed by fish and breadcrumbs vanished with amazing speed under that stove.

Intermittent curses gave way to an unsteady rumble, punctuated by woo-oo's and a hacking cough.

At last the creature emerged, came unsteadily to me, sinking on my feet. I stroked him; he did not cringe. He seemed to press his body against my hand. He who had crept into the house to die was mine, dead or alive.

"It's all right, Woo. This is your home."

I gave him to the golden Nada, whose maternal love was sure. She lay before the fire, nursing Woo in her groin and they slept for an hour.

Timothy Woo, as he became, at least six years old, was safely in his first home, and happy—so happy.

I never understood why my animals accepted him so readily from the beginning; all save two black and white cats. Those, Bijou and her daughter, Panda, gave piercing shrieks whenever they met the crooked one. He did leer at them, whirring and woo-ing, and eventually gave chase, I believe only for the joy of hearing those shrieks.

At first I gave him a day or two to live. He was a carcass strung together by lank fur. Since his first visit he must have been caught in a trap for longer than I cared to consider. The marks were on his legs, barely healed over.

Gradually signs of vitality grew. It was a fortnight before he could stretch and yawn in the manner of all satisfied cats. His chest remained wheezily imperfect.

In a household where other human beings had to be considered too, it soon became apparent that something would have to be done. Timothy Woo ignored the bare decencies of life. The house began to smell.

There was only one thing to be done. A major operation, at his age, ensued. There was a slight risk, the vet said, because he had only one lung. Shuddering at the alternative, I said: "Operate."

On the day of his operation I was kept busy at a Chamber of Commerce, reporter's notebook in hand. It was imperative that I missed no spoken word, and a miracle that I did not. Voices flew in cajolery, dreary explanation and thunder.

I found this free-lance reporting and secretarial work enlightening. It gave me brief insight into trades and professions of which, otherwise, I should have remained ignorant. Reporting could be a frightening business but—mine own! I could type back the voluminous notes at speed, and in my natural element: cats on shoulders, dogs at my feet; I had to work hard to keep them all.

My only stock-in-trade was reliability. That included promptness, amiability under the most trying conditions and, above all, accuracy.

Usually I was able to lean across to the Secretary and whisper: "That was Mr. . . ? Yes, of course."

On that particular day the Secretary whispered to me: "You needn't take this long speech down. I can give it to you verbatim afterwards."

I refrained from throwing grateful arms round his neck. "Shall I have time to telephone? My—next client is anxious to hear from me."

"Certainly. He's a slow speaker and it will be half an hour at least."

I tore to the telephone. The line was engaged. I waited, then had a wrong number. My agitation would have been unbearable but for the fact that a man was still speaking laboriously. At last I was through.

Clenching my sticky palm against Button A, I swallowed before speaking.

"Can you tell me, please—*please* can you tell me—how is Timothy Woo?"

He was conscious, safe, and ready for me to collect. I went back to that wretched board-room to give a more accurately detailed report than ever before.

I grasped Timothy Woo to my bosom on the way home, and typed from chloroform-scented notes for the rest of the evening.

He grew stronger and ever more devoted. Through a sea of well-bred and fabulously good-looking animals a crooked face emerged, always first to reach me. One eye up, one down, and ears lopping forward, the rest of his face had lost its painful grin. His body now was the shape of a cat's and life glowed in the tabby pattern.

From a perfectly wild cat, suspicious of and unused to the human touch, he became a model of all domestic creatures. Resented by none of them, except the two black and white cats, he soon took on extraordinary responsibilities. Visitors would remark: "Why ever did you choose such an ugly cat?"

"I didn't. He chose me."

To say that Timothy Woo shared my life and anxieties would be to underrate his esoteric qualities. He anticipated events. He read thoughts; he must have done.

On one occasion I brought the horses in at night earlier than usual. I wanted them and their tack to be shining and bright for the following morning, so set to work. I brushed, rubbed, polished and polished again. Nothing was forgotten. Nothing?

"Woo-oo."

"I shan't be long, Timothy Woo. You'll be fed with the others in due course."

"Woo-oo." This time he wandered towards the paddock, woo-ing and turning back for me. So plaintive became his wheezed call that, at last, I followed him.

"You don't want to go out there. Dinner!"

That was not the point. He went on, came back for me then sprang forward again. Curious, I followed to the centre of a darkening field. He sat down, making the same ridiculous noise. I picked him up and would have carried him home, but for the language he turned out. Springing from my arms, he went back to the same spot and—sat down. Then, nosing the ground, he looked up at me. The message in those uneven eyes was not clear; only the anguish in them.

17

I tried to pick him up again but he moved aside. My hand touched something cold. As I picked it up to examine, he rubbed against my legs with a marked: "Perrow-woo-oo."

"But it *can't* be. They were both shod this week."

The horseshoe in my hand felt ominously new. I went back to the stable, following Timothy Woo, and found that, sure enough, Ballygiblin had on three new shoes. The fourth was in my hand.

Another time I found my pony with a nasty gash above the fetlock. Timothy Woo, as usual, was with me; so were the dogs.

I hurried back to the house with the dogs, thinking that Timothy Woo would follow in due course. Not he! By the time I reached the telephone he was there, right under the instrument, looking at me anxiously.

On another occasion he fetched me to the telephone; back and forth he prowled until I obeyed. The receiver was hanging down with the resultant crackling sound.

As a midwife he really excelled himself. Nada's second litter was late and troublesome. It is a lamented fact with vets that too often they are sought at midnight. Perhaps the thought of approaching small hours saps courage and reason. I glanced at Timothy Woo, the only other person present. He curled round and feigned sleep, the eye at higher level remaining half-shut. I decided against telephoning.

I nodded and dozed. The retriever became less restless. At three a.m. Timothy Woo sprang to attention, for no apparent reason.

The first puppy was born within ten minutes, more suddenly than usual. The next hours were busy. There was trouble with the sixth puppy. Then three were born in quick succession, and that seemed to be that.

Leaving Nada comfortable, I went to fetch her warm milk. When I went back I was appalled to see Timothy Woo, who had been in one position all night, leaning over the basket and scooping nine puppies towards the mother's chest. Then I understood.

Another puppy, the last, was on its way. As usual the earlier arrivals had pushed tailwards. Nada was in no way perturbed that the cat had carried on where I left off.

Timothy Woo and Nada brought that litter up between them.

He lived with me for three and a half years and never attained visible beauty, but he changed considerably. Although his coat shone, he could never lose a constant leer caused by a permanently raised lip. That and his delicate chest condition remained with him.

But the strain of human unconcern, or worse, had been erased by his few happy years.

We fought the disabilities for as long as we could. It left me with frightening vet bills, but with something else too.

The day came when all the drugs and veterinary ability could do no more. We had always been honest with each other, Timothy Woo and I.

My hand caressed his head while he waited for the blessed needle to arrive. "Timothy Woo, I'm *sorry* I can't do any more for you."

Relaxed, he waited patiently in my arms, fully alert, pressing his body as close to mine as he could.

I talked to him while we waited, so that smoothness of voice might allay possible fear.

"Do you know, Timothy Woo, I'm tired of board-rooms and committee meetings. I should like to live near woods, or the sea, or where a brook chatters all day. I want to write. Do you suppose I could?"

Without a tremble he watched my face as the car drew up and I went on talking. I don't know what I said. Those crooked eyes never faltered in their gaze as I spoke to the vet. Her verdict was the same as mine.

Timothy Woo made one slight move as his release approached. It was not a struggle. He reached up with two forepaws, still marked by a vicious trap, and touched my face. It was the overwhelming gesture of deep knowledge and assurance.

It was over. I lit a cigarette, thanked the vet and showed her out.

Although I missed him sorely, I never mope over dead animals, especially when I know they have had the best I can give them. I think their memory should be worn with a light touch; not as a pall to be paraded before our unfortunate relatives and friends.

Who are we to say what is over and finished, and what is not?

Exactly a year later I wandered up to the loft in the evening. It happened to be my birthday, that is why I recall it so precisely. The loft is a light, airy room and pleasant in the summer.

My vague wish to become a writer was coupled, as it is too often, with lack of courage to start. The vagueness was turning into a must. I must start some day.

With no deeper reason I cleared a table up there, fetched my typewriter and wrote: "CHAPTER ONE". Then I went into the garden to think.

The next day, with growing determination, I telephoned an agent and several friends. The gist of my messages was that, as from the second week in June, I should be "away" for two months. I just hoped that my secretariat business would survive. It did.

Then I went to the loft, feeling much as those must have done who once "walked the plank", and sat down at the typewriter.

I wrote the first paragraph, which still exists—in print. I worked there for most of the day and, by bed time, had written and re-written a thousand words.

That which I had achieved in one day could be repeated the next day. Then I wrote two thousand words. That is the goal I set myself, and kept to it.

I soon found that mornings and late into the night were my best times for writing. On the third night I was tired but happy. I had created a situation revolving round several characters. Could I sustain it?

What a fool I was to have cancelled business appointments and turned down new contacts. The thought removed much happiness.

A sound, for no apparent reason, crept through a weary mind to my ears. In memory I heard a whirring "Woo-oo!"

From that night my resolve never faltered. I finished my first novel in just under three months from the day I started it. Eventually it was published. I have had many more published since then.

But, as other writers will know, success did not come overnight, nor in that first year. Authors, like stray cats, need layers and layers of courage. On top of those a suit of steel armour and, lest that should crack, an air-tight, water-tight, failure-tight covering of grim determination.

Chapter Two

As soon as my first book was published and my second written, I felt a wild surge towards freedom.

Writing was to make the world my oyster. And I needed only a tiny portion of the world to live in. I was not to know then that writing becomes more difficult as one proceeds.

I had to wait a week or so until Nada's puppies were fully weaned and then I called the dogs together in conference.

It was early June; just the time to take a holiday or, for that matter, create a new life. In such a spirit of vague optimism I prepared my Ford van, so ideally equipped with space and windows, for a jaunt into the blue.

I had discussed the matter fully with my mother, who was in the same frame of mind: why live in the centre of England at all, when the shores had so much sea and beauty to recommend them?

Ignoring my cautious demon, who whispered horrid things about having no private income or security, I was ready to set off with three dogs; Nada, Bracken and the terrier, Snip. They were barking joyfully because they had grasped my mood. Eagerly they watched me pile in blankets, ground sheet, frying-pan, dog dishes, odds and ends, and a map.

Nada didn't mind leaving behind one puppy by then. She knew that it would be well cared for. But just as we were setting off a letter arrived from a friend whom I had not seen for years. She and her family lived in mid-Wales. She had heard that I had golden retriever puppies, and wondered if there might be one left.

So the puppy was added to the bouncing van-load, and we set off to deliver her safely. That is how I came to inspect properties in the Cardiganshire area.

Our warm greetings at the puppy's new home were unsurpassed; so was the incredible beauty of our surroundings. A solid grey farmhouse, resting among mountains and miles from any other building, was a wonderful place to meet old friends.

If this were mid-Wales, then let me see more of it. Next day, refreshed in mind and body, I set off to interview estate agents.

My vague request for a picturesque spot in which I could live, write and keep a few pets, produced weird and unsuitable results. For two days I inspected gloomy bungalows in forgotten side lanes, ugly farmhouses with ten acres or so, or "something more compact"—meaning some gaunt horror cheek by jowl with its twin in a village.

I sighed for Warwickshire lanes, wondering why I had come so far. A heat-wave produced intense longing for glades beside flowing water. In such a spot, with the dogs roaming freely, I would laze and dream; dream of a sequestered cottage leaning against a hillside in the privacy of its own acres. There would be the music of a bubbling brook below the cottage and a whispering forest near by.

Glancing at the estate agent's list, I realized that I had seen all but one of the properties offered. It was becoming too hot to inspect another, which was sure to be a replica of those I'd seen: stark isolation and absurd inconveniences.

"Pant Glas", I read. The figure asked was above that of a simple cottage. But if all those acres went with it then, although cheap, it must be arid and gloomy. The thing to do was to drive on to a pleasant and solitary camping-site.

"You'd like that, dogs, wouldn't you?" They were growing restless. Bracken whined and Snip barked. Perhaps it was time to pull up and give them a run.

To reach a destination which I had in mind I had to pass through the village where Pant Glas hid, empty but freehold. I slowed down, glancing casually at a village which probably I should never see again. It was an ordinary grey village, ugly by Cotswold standards.

I was about to accelerate when the dogs went frantic. Possibly the act of slowing down the car had deluded them. So I pulled up, away from the main road, saying: "All right. I suppose you must. But I can't take you over private land. Wait a minute; I'll look round."

I expect she who leaned over her white gate thought I was crazy, talking to myself. As I wound down my window she gave me the sweetest smile and we exchanged greetings. I asked where Pant Glas was. She pointed to a path opposite.

"That's it. And there now, a lovely walk it is."

Eyeing the rising hill, I asked: "Is it far?"

"Not so far, and your dogs will love it. Pant Glas means *Green Valley*, you know. Or there, I suppose Blue Valley it is, really."

How right she was in all respects! The dogs raced headlong up the steep rise to a new paradise. It *was* green; it *was* blue.

The first wide field was fringed by silver birches to the west, larches to the east. Their blue shadows rested on deep green grass which had not been disturbed by cattle for some long time.

A hare darted from one covert to another for the dogs' enjoyment. By the time they rejoined me I had reached a welcome brook. Leaping downhill over grey and white stones, it cascaded in foam to a deeper sport below the larches. Crystal clear, it wore fern and wild flowers on either bank.

Above me, still upwards, a stony path lay beneath the leisurely shade of interlaced leaves. Whoever had lived in such arcadia had not troubled over-much about wheeled transport, I decided.

I began to look ahead for—surely?—a large house. But only wide fields rising to oak woods, with the tip of mountains showing beyond, were there.

Suddenly, to my left, I saw a little white cottage. Possibly a gamekeeper's lodge or cowman's home? Still I gazed ahead expectantly, but soon turned to the cottage, realizing that it must be the only building there.

There were several outbuildings beside the double-fronted cottage. Beyond it and supported by the dwelling was a tumbled-down wood shed. Snip approved of that greatly. She pushed through the half open door to tear joyfully at loose earth. She had not behaved like that at the other properties I had inspected. So thoroughly did she dig and scratch that she might have been laying a foundation stone—and probably was!

From the boulder step in front of the door I looked at the rolling landscape beyond and was thrilled to see the sea glinting back at me through the near-by forest leaves.

The retrievers sniffed madly everywhere, at last enticing me up the wooded knoll, against which the cottage seemed to *grow*.

From the top of the knoll a new world opened to my astonished gaze. Across the Dovey Estuary, and reflected in a still sea, was Aberdovey, white and blue. The hills beyond it, reaching to the stupendous roll of mountains, were alight with gorse in full bloom.

I could not know then, as I stood spellbound, that other view points on Pant Glas land continued the vistas in exciting serial form.

The dogs bounded back to the boulder step, I following no less eagerly.

I stared again at the cottage, resting beneath its wooded hillside, like a white leghorn, its windowed eyes blinking complacently at the sun.

I listened to the brook chattering as it passed by below. I watched yellow-hammers, blue-tits and scores of various birds hovering in and around the small garden.

To my right was a gate and beyond it the forest *sang*. There was no breeze that day to stir the trees to a rustle or, as I was to discover later, to a full orchestral furore. Then it seemed that every branch held a bird and each bird was in full song.

At last, ignoring the pleading in three pairs of eyes, I closed a wooden gate, which had swung open towards a neglected garden, before moving away. If it were mine I should do that, I thought.

If it were mine!

I strolled back to the van, idling past blue shadows and green banks to the lower fields. There the illusion was such that I could pick up an azure sea in cupped hands. The ochre bogland below was mixed with coral, olive and palest lime greens. Above it curlews called incessantly.

I forgot my dream for a time. Obviously my mother, then in her seventieth year, would not care to live above the world before her time, even in such a tranquil haven.

There was no road or path from the village to the cottage. There was a well but no mod. cons. We knew no local inhabitants; they might not care for us—intruders.

There were ninety-nine reasons why I could never live at Pant Glas. It was useless considering mid-Wales, where the country ran up and down—mostly up. As they say in Cardiganshire: "You go up on your head and down on your head."

It would be of no use looking at further properties. So I took the dogs to a peaceful site near Dolgelly where perfect freedom reigned.

We spent three days and nights there before I returned home to make the regretted announcement: it was not practical to live in Wales.

Chapter Three

FROM the moment I returned home from the journey which included my first glimpse of Pant Glas, I noticed a different attitude among the animals. This impression was borne in upon me by slow degrees.

The days of Timothy Woo were long past. My last pekinese had died of old age. Because Snip regarded that breed as a joke at both ends, I did not replace. I suppose for an intelligent terrier to be unable to discern whether a dog of her own size was coming or going *was* disconcerting.

We had only two cats, Michael and Panda. Their stares grew different. Whether from slit or wide open eyes, an inscrutable watching campaign developed.

Whatever news they had gleaned from the dogs, by scent or sound, went deep. They sat in different places from usual and were in the house more often.

It is an accepted fact that animals warn each other. Those who follow hounds know what to expect when a jay cries. The fox is duly warned by his friend with the better view point. The jay doesn't leave it there. His varied cries must mean: "Stay where you are." "Come out now and run into the wind." "Now then, hounds are running from the west. Cross the stream, double back and follow me."

The jay has a varied vocabulary which the most seasoned huntsman cannot interpret. But it is effective.

So do hedgehogs, and the more helpless creatures, take good heed of the pip-pipped warning note of the blackbird. Sometimes hedge sparrows join in.

When I take dogs through the forest on a warm summer's evening, it is not without some fear. I call or whistle, not for the dogs' benefit but to warn their likely prey that danger is on its way. Often when my warning is too late and the dogs are hunting like mad, the "pip-pip-pip . . . pip-pip" takes over for me.

We know how animals, especially dogs, greet each other, pleasantly or otherwise. A tensed body and rigid tail often augur ill for the oncomer.

Then it seems reasonable to believe that warnings and greetings are not the only forms of animal converse. To those which live with us we are the source of perpetual and intense interest. We observe their peculiarities, they ours. And they certainly discuss among themselves, often anticipate, many of our movements.

So when I say that the dogs thoroughly talked over their journey and its certain consequences—certain to them— with the cats, I don't think I'm talking nonsense.

I believe, too, that cats are more patient and accurate relaters. Where dogs rush up to greet and are on to the next interest, cats meander.

The horses knew something in next to no time. That isn't remarkable, because Michael, the tabby, slept on my old hunter on summer nights. Often, in the early morning, there was the dew-imprinted shape of the family gossiper.

Long after the *silent ones* had talked and talked, I began to think of the dream place I had seen in Wales. It clarified only when I mentioned it in passing for the first time.

For, from the moment I had left those bewitching slopes, I had tucked Pant Glas at the back of my mind, much as one dismisses a beautiful dream.

And so at the beginning the miracle evolved with little human management. Born and bred in the Midland shires, there was no apparent reason why it grew suddenly imperative that my mother and I should live in Wales. Her inclinations suddenly veered in that direction, apart from my own.

"It would be rather nice to live near the sea," she remarked. "Didn't you see *anything* possible in Wales?"

"I think it would be too hilly for you, dear. There *was* one place but—no, it wouldn't do for you."

The dogs watched. Two cats listened; one sharpened his claws on a log before strolling out, merging his long shadow with those spreading before a full moon. There is more to know and more to tell when the moon is full.

And so a series of trivial promptings drifted into mild action. An estate agent friend was persuaded to glance at the one property I had partly approved. Partly!

I went with him, more for the swift joy of glimpsing paradise again, than from any practical reason. He had told me to look for a house or cottage with a sound roof.

He agreed: the roof was sound. From his expression, as his car refused the final rise, I gathered that his opinion of my mental state was not similar.

We prowled, we poked, we pushed. His penknife was thrust into beams, making no remarkable impression. We walked round the sunlit acres and back to the cottage. His eyes seemed fatally cast earthwards.

"Are you looking for drains?"

"*Drains*—in Wales? You want a lot for your money."

"It isn't damp, is it?" I suggested, idiotically. It was the third week of a heat-wave so nothing was damp.

The first note of enthusiasm, which I was quick to detect, crept into his reply: "No, I should say it's never damp. That's one of the odd things about this place."

"One of them?" I asked in a flat voice. "You don't think it will do?" With foregone conclusion, I added: "You think . . . ?"

He stared at me. "I think you're as mad as a hatter. But it's the loveliest spot I've ever seen. If you don't have it, I rather think I shall."

Had he been single and I a blushing girl of seventeen he could not have set my pulse racing more madly. "But how should we get to the cottage? There's no path."

"That's easy. You'd make one. You'd have to get a Land-Rover or jeep. Your mother *might* like it."

"She might not. Don't persuade her."

"Don't worry, I shan't," he said grimly. "But, at the right price, it's—it's worth considering."

He repeated that last remark when we gave a faithful report to my mother. The *pros* were faint; the *cons* stuck out a mile. But he admitted that Pant Glas certainly had charm—an elusive something.

My mother said quietly: "Charm should be elusive. I'd rather like to see Pant Glas, even if we don't have it."

During that conversation tails were beating a steady tattoo on the carpet. The cats washed their faces, in readiness for the great move three months later.

Snip, discoverer of Pant Glas

Three golden generations: Nada, Bracken and Sheena

Co-operation at the eleventh hour

Never be misled by a sanctimonious expression

Belinda, of all the goats her sense of humour equals Siriol's

From that moment she was one of them

Now Sylvan towers over the rest of the herd

Nada, counting her chickens

Often it is Jane who tells the goats to take courage

A case of divide and rule for Archibald II (*below*) and Pewter

The beautiful Mrs. Henry Wood and the others didn't stand a chance beside Fanny

Anything young comes under Nada's care

Siriol's sense of humour is highly developed, but dry

Cardigan Pride, a perfect chestnut filly

This is Bess, Siriol; she's yours

Family in full cry

Nada, Sheena and Snip pretend to kill Bracken, who loves it

Nada investigates

Is she going away?

Chita, a dedicated and determined mother

Some of Chita's family . . .

. . . about to drop in to lunch

Out in the paddock the old bay hunter, Ballygiblin, blew heavily into night grass, clearing his nostrils of pollen. His shadow, an aged Welsh pony, moved stiffly at his side. The terrible decision was mine, not theirs.

I evaded the issue for as long as I could. I knew that the pony's days were heavily numbered, but I had transport laid on for the horse in his twenty-ninth year. I fought my conscience for a long time, until within five days of leaving Warwickshire. And then I knew that I must pay the price.

I had proposed taking my gallant friend, from the plain and rolling countryside he loved and knew so intimately, to end his days among hills and mountains.

It's so easy to persuade oneself. But at heart I knew that I was asking a great gentleman, who had given brilliant and active service all his life, to live out his days in boredom —and without his constant friend, the pony. Already the slight rises in Warwickshire tried his stiffening legs.

That which I had preached so often must now be put into practice: when old and useful horses grow beyond the work they know, it is a mistaken sense of kindness to leave them to stand and stare, alone. Whether in a stable, field or on windswept moor, old age applies its cruel penances, which only humanity should be expected to endure.

Why didn't I get a younger horse or pony to keep him company? I answered that question many times, even to horse lovers.

An old horse can be irritated by youth in numerous ways. How would Ballygiblin feel when he watched me lead a younger mount from his side, saddle up and ride away? He, who had never refused or fallen, would have nothing to do but watch his own shadow on the grass.

The next morning, in brilliant sunshine, I led him out of the field, groomed him, spoke cheerfully, and took him to the familiar mounting block. There a man with humane killer acted instantly.

There was the same treatment for the pony, who had been left well out of sight and sound.

I seemed in that instant to have left Warwickshire for ever. When actually I did leave there were no false regrets as I looked at the empty paddock. I was glad that I had found enough courage to render ultimate service to two dear friends who had never stinted theirs.

So when the dogs and I were the advance guard of the stupendous move-in to Pant Glas, its rolling acres were strangely empty of livestock. The furniture and cats followed me. My mother, happily, came two days later.

It was stupendous for several reasons, not least the fact that we set off in a thick fog, although it was early October.

I had been persuaded to let the two cats travel in the van, rather than share a packed Land-Rover with three dogs. It was a choice which I regretted later in the day.

It took three hours to travel the first fifty miles. During that time I waited many times for the van to roll slowly into view. I had several reassuring talks with the cats who, to my horror, had been placed on the back of the van, their cages lightly swathed with tarpaulin.

Eventually the van driver suggested that I should go on and open up the cottage in readiness for them.

Due to reach Pant Glas at midday, the van arrived in full

moonlight at ten in the evening. It had suffered a series of punctures and burst tires.

The dogs were beside themselves with joy at their second sight of the place they had originally chosen. Nada took her daughter, Bracken, sniffing over knoll and fields. Snip, astounded to see her wood shed converted into a writing-room, complete with many windows, sought vermin elsewhere.

My harassed thoughts were only of missing cats. I pictured them lost, stolen and strayed anywhere between the Midlands and Cardigan Bay. Eventually I went to the nearest telephone, a mile away, to discover the reason for such delay.

I was assured that the cats had been safely with the van at four o'clock in the afternoon, when spare tires had been sent out to it. But they would be hungry and terrified, despite their light doping.

Worse was to come. The removal man came at nine-thirty in the evening to announce that the van was not far behind. He had come on by car, but hadn't thought of bringing the cats on with him. They were safe, he said.

Although a kind neighbour had given permission for the van to cross his fields, because of my difficult path which had been cut only two days ago, no persuasion would induce the driver to go farther than the village below; so far below.

It would take a whole day to remove the contents from the van to my vehicle, which was the only alternative.

I was a stranger in a strange land, so had no friends to call upon. I had discounted the spirit of my new village, Tre'r-Ddol.

The van pulled up. Above the sound of its engine I heard Michael's plaintive protests and Panda's thinner miaow.

While men went into gloomy consultation about heights, bumps and sinister curves of land, I swept the cats in their cages up to the cottage, where the dogs shrieked welcome. Pushing food in to them, I left the cats prisoners and returned to the fray.

To my amazement, the village had turned out to a man. The nearest farmer, without demur, brought out his Land-Rover, stripped its roof and mine.

"Leave it to us. We'll get you in." And they did.

All night long those two vehicles plied up and down the quarter of a mile of rocky surface, crammed with furniture and willing helpers.

Small boys footed it, carrying remarkable burdens to ease the loads. There must have been many tolerant wives and mothers in Tre'r-Ddol that night.

At one-thirty in the morning I cooked the largest mixed grill I had produced in my life. Bacon, sausages, eggs and the contents of many tins sizzled and were eaten in no time. Mugs, cups, basins of tea were swallowed in right good spirit. The barn-cum-kitchen resembled a riotous inn on New Year's Eve.

"What's this, Miss—a gramophone?"

"Not—er—exactly. I think we'll have that in the far bedroom."

Below in the village the kind Mrs. Vearey, who had told me in June that Pant Glas meant Blue or Green Valley, worked hard. She and her two sisters set up an emergency café, supplying free refreshments to the loaders.

I have never seen such incredible enthusiasm, good spirits and efficiency. By four o'clock in the morning farmers and foresters, who had to be up at dawn, wished me genially: "Good night, Miss Williams. Let us know if we can do anything."

Suddenly I stood in the stillness of a furnished cottage, waving farewell to the removal men. They had remained good-tempered throughout, buoyed up by the wonderfully co-operative spirit they had found in a small, Welsh village.

Abashed at having caused so much chaos, I stood on the boulder step, watching moonlight shimmering on a dark blue sea. The hills and fields could be seen in clear shape, if not in detail.

When physical tiredness was held in check by wonder at so much beauty around, I knew I had come—home. I was amongst friends, not strangers. So, indeed, it proved.

Because on a June morning the dogs had insisted that I should dally where they chose, now I was about to spend my first night, or what remained of it, as a Welsh landowner—near the sea.

And near the woods, and where a brook chattered incessantly.

And I was a writer.

As I turned to go indoors the forest stirred faintly, as a sleeper will sigh before waking.

The dogs were unconscious on familiar rugs. I went upstairs to share a confusion of bedding with two thankful cats.

Chapter Four

BECAUSE there was much to be done by way of getting straight, the exquisite pleasure of Pant Glas was borne in by degrees. The cottage lies in the middle of its generous acres, which consist of *below* and *above*. There are a few level areas.

I would rush in: "Mother, do you know, we own a silver birch coppice and a large field beyond the oak woods." Or: "There are *five* acres of knoll behind us, not two." Land is measured under the sky in these parts.

We had been here only eight days when the goats arrived.

"I certainly hadn't thought of keeping goats. For one thing, I can't milk."

Such mild protest was useless. The kind friends, to whom I had given the golden retriever puppy in June—thus leading to my discovery of Pant Glas—were so grateful. They wanted to do something for me. They did.

I agreed to try out their generous gift of the goats for a day or so. There were three: Niall (pronounced Neal), a pure white British Saarnen, and her two daughters who were horned, and sired by a famous Anglo-Nubian.

Belinda, the dark brown one with floppy ears, and her twin, Bambi, rubbed affectionately with their horns in my ribs when I called to take them over on trial.

"Trial" was the key word. They travelled twelve miles in

the Land-Rover very well, coaxed by nicotine. I had to chain smoke all the way home, blowing puffs over my shoulder at regular intervals.

Niall's white beard tickled the nape of my neck as she bent forward solemnly to inhale. Then, closing her eyes in ecstasy, she would throw back her head and breathe: "A-aah!" The others did the same.

By the time we reached Pant Glas I knew something about goats. There was more to learn.

Happily, their owner's children had come with them to see them settled in. They gave me my first arduous milking lesson.

The question of free range or tethering arose. I agreed to play for safety the first day. After that collars and bells would have to suffice. At least I should know where they were. No creature was going to be imprisoned by a chain on my premises.

With two people to hang on to each goat, I did manage to extract some milk. They promised airily that I would soon become an adept milker. Let the goats nibble a handful of hay while I milked, they said. And then those charming, callous youngsters left me.

I looked into the goats' implacable eyes and wanted to scream after my departing visitors: "Come back! Take them with you." It was too late; they had gone.

I loved the goats. My fear was that they wouldn't stand to be milked and would suffer accordingly.

Somewhere I had a book on goats. I turned out drawers and cupboards until it was found and avidly read. The technical information grew more and more alarming. My stable was

39

utterly inadequate. It had no divisions, slatted floor, benches or a score of recommended accessories.

Then I turned to a chapter on feeding, which l decidedly shaken. The goats would starve before I coul what they needed. Such foods as Maize Gluten Feed, Coombs, Weatings, Coco-nut cake, and so on, dazed untutored brain.

By the time I had read a chapter on ailments, my mind was made up: I was no fit person to keep goats. I went out to tell them so, and to apologize. But they looked so happy, I hadn't the heart to say anything then. Instead, I released their chains so that they could wander freely for a time.

Such unaccustomed freedom went to their heads. They bustled off up the fields, then bustled back again. Their gratitude was overwhelming; I must reward it. I found matches in my pocket but, curiously, no cigarettes. A pity, because I was going to blow smoke over them.

They were away again, Niall gulping and chewing as she went. A nasty suspicion dawned. I felt in my pocket again and tore after her. By the time I reached her only a scrap of tobacco hung from her mouth. She had eaten a packet of twenty cigarettes, and the tin-foil.

As evening approached my problem was how to get them in. Happily I had flaked maize, so lured them with that. The others took their cue from Niall. Once the stable door was shut I faced the problem of milking.

Calmly I fetched a bucket and sat on a stool by Niall. Her saintly expression was reassuring. I began to milk, slowly. Four squirts and I was flat on my back, the bucket upturned in my lap. A rodeo ensued.

An hour and a half later I returned to the house with a breakfast-cup of milk and several bruises. The next morning the combined quantity of their milk was slightly larger; so were my bruises.

Perhaps a day's freedom would make them more amenable. I had been told by their owner, whom they adored, that he wasn't getting more than two pints from the three of them at that time of year. As to food, he had assured me over the telephone, he never gave them anything other than a little hay at night.

Consoled, I faced the night's milking with more equanimity. But Niall wouldn't stand. She bounced, cavorted and leapt. When anchored by a short chain, she bucked and reared. Eventually I struggled out with nearly a pint of milk, from the three.

They were so happy, even at milking times. And friendly. No longer troubled by heavy weights to prevent their wandering, they spent three deliriously contented days and nights before I knew that I must send them back.

If I was to go on writing I couldn't spend three hours a day milking three ungrateful goats. I adored seeing them about the place but —there it was—back they must go.

I said all that, adding: "It's such a pity, because this place calls out for goats. It has rough grazing, pasture, gorse bushes, plenty of water and good fencing. What fools they are!"

I watched Michael's tabby form wander up the knoll. He went straight to the goats, rubbing affectionately against Belinda's leg.

"Even the cat likes them. Tomorrow I must phone and take them back."

It would mean a daily journey to the village to fetch milk, but that would be quicker and far less painful than being hurtled round the stable by demented demons.

That night I went into battle for the last time. As I was taking them back first thing in the morning, their owner could milk them out if I failed. No great harm would have been done—to the goats. I rubbed my painful shoulder thoughtfully.

Taking a deep breath I went into the stable, shutting myself in with the beloved enemy. I wasn't going to be misled by their sanctimonious expressions, or gentle nosings in my pockets.

I put Niall into her milking position by the door and sat on the stool beside her. This was going to hurt me more than it hurt her. I grasped the teats, trying not to let the tremble of anticipation reach my hands.

Swish, swish—milk, milk, milk. I couldn't believe it. There she stood, with an expression slightly more benign than the Mona Lisa, but just as inscrutable, letting me extract the last drop from her generous udder; three and a half pints!

I thanked her, stroked her and set her free. Now for her dangerous daughters.

It was the same with Belinda, who gave me two pints with the gracious benevolence of a duchess opening a bazaar.

Bambi began by shuffling about a bit. She was soon chastized by her mother, who butted her in the ribs. Half-way through a most satisfactory milking she raised a foot. Niall bit her ear. From that moment Bambi was a model of perfection. The result was three pints.

"You darlings! Have you—decided to stay?"

Niall pressed her head lovingly into my stomach and gave

her low chuckle, for which she is renowned. Was she saying that I'd passed the test? Perhaps by next morning they would have reverted to type.

Not they. From that moment I had not the slightest trouble with the trio as regards milking. Although winter was approaching their output increased, due, I was told, to the fact that I gave them concentrates morning and evening. That, free-range grazing, plus a little hay in bad weather and profound contentment were the answer. Our friendship ripened quickly.

They had all been in milk for nearly three years, I was told. Naturally they would soon be dry. The only profound truth I have learned about goats in the subsequent five years is that— no law governs them.

You can read or write as many handbooks as you will on goats. Every single statement can be contradicted by someone's goats somewhere. Goat keepers and vets whom I have consulted on the subject are agreed on that point. General rules may be applied, but there are always an alarming number of exceptions.

"They'll ruin all your trees," *they* said. Nothing of the sort. My oaks, silver birch and larches remain unhurt. They did make a nasty mess of two apple-trees by thoroughly barking them when they broke into the garden. But Welsh plum-trees are a dish they hold in absolute contempt.

Those three goats went on giving a generous milk supply, a gallon a day in winter and two throughout the following summer. I think they would have gone on much longer had I not at last had them mated.

A full moon affects them strangely. It seems that they can't bear to waste a moment of it, winter or summer. They hold butting matches, push and shove competitions, and the younger ones—now that goats swarm over Pant Glas—love nothing better than to stand on the ridge of the cottage roof, an alarming height above the ground.

Visitors often find this disconcerting. The approach to Pant Glas, especially by moonlight, affects people in various ways:

"What a wonderful walk!"

"So glad I could bring the car up. I should have been terrified on foot."

"We thought the house would never appear."

"Moonlight on the sea—how romantic!"

Or, as on one memorable evening, when friends—one of psychic tendencies—arrived on foot in the moonlight, that frightful scream. I rushed out to find the screamer fainting in her husband's arms.

"Not her *ankle*?" I asked with concern.

"No, your ancestors, or hers," he remarked drily.

My gaze followed his. Etched against a night-blue sky, their reflections silver on a dark roof, stood six goatlings nose to tail. One with horns, all with beards, their symmetry was unique but sinister.

She soon revived, murmuring: "It's an omen!"

How we laughed when the statues sprang into the air, with double twists, disappearing on to the raised bank beyond the building!

Gradually Niall and her daughters gave a valuable herd to the estate, Niall remaining solemnly their leader. It is registered as The Dovey Herd. The bells they wear, in slightly varying tones, are pleasing and useful. Wanderers are quickly detected.

At times we might be in the heart of the Bernese Oberland, especially when rare snow tops distant mountains. Bells chime in the foreground or tinkle in the far distance. They have even been confused with the Bells of Aberdovey. That is probably wishful thinking, but never have I wished my beloved goats at the bottom of the sea!

They are lovable pets. Gentle and gracious, independent too, they are easy to handle. Their herd instinct is strong and their leader infallible, to them. But on occasions, especially on a sunny March day, they can be devils incarnate. Then it is easy to understand the Biblical comparison between the sheep and the goats.

You go out to milk one morning as usual and no goat is in sight. After an hour's searching there is only one possible conclusion: an air lift.

On one such occasion I went round all forestry fencing with minute care. Then my own inter-fencing with an adjoining farm showed no sign for alarm. There must be a solution. There was.

Having examined all wire fences with a precision worthy of Sherlock Holmes, I then took stock of the ground on the farther side, although the ground was hard. There were no hoof prints or freshly disturbed earth.

Then, because I was writing, or should have been writing, an almost clueless thriller, I worked on different lines. If I were a goat how would I get to the other side? From raised ground, of course.

I had tramped another mile before I realized that, not far below the cottage, the bank by the stream was almost as high as the fence some four feet away from it. It would be a difficult jump for a horse; worse for a goat, or nine goats, with udders.

But there I found three white hairs on top of the fencing.

As I crossed fields towards the Clettwyr, a tumbling river which names its fascinating valley, I much regretted having removed the goats' collars. There had been good reason for this. Tasty spring shoots on tall trees and bushes tempted them. There was danger of hanging, and although I muttered imprecations under my breath, that is not the end I would choose for them. That day, as I tramped for fruitless miles, I told myself that I could willingly have hanged the lot of them!

The next day I found them, having started off early on horseback to continue the search. Uncomfortably overdue for milking, they lolled on a green sward less than two miles from home, as the crow flies.

With only one steep hill between their point of escape and capture, they must have bobbed over the brow when they saw me coming, then bobbed back again. Had it not been for their painful udders, we might have played that game indefinitely.

"Niall, you wicked old sinner!"

"Miar-aair."

Meekly she followed the cob, the others taking their cue from her. For safety I slipped on their collars and bells. We positively chimed our way through the village, where my eccentricities by then were cheerfully accepted. Who, they ask, other than a writer would keep a herd of goats? Anyone but a writer, I should say.

But I *like* goats. The genuine excuses I could, and do sometimes, offer are only to placate those well-meaning folk who advise me on different lines.

Since keeping them neither my mother nor I have had a twinge of rheumatism, which used to attack us in varying degrees.

They supply more than enough milk for our needs the year round. The surplus is never wasted. Dogs, cats, poultry and all young creatures thrive on it.

They are rough grazers and love the long, withered grass which horses and sheep despise. Their manure is also of great value.

But it strikes me as being a curious insistence that all animals should be *useful*. Their various uses can always *be* named. But suppose the same criterion were demanded of the human race, or else . . . ?

When I sell puppies there are several stock questions which alarm me, often to the extent of avoiding a sale:

"It must be a good house-dog."

There is nothing more to be avoided than a perpetual yapper or barker. A nice, sharp bark when the door is knocked, nine times out of ten means a cheerful welcome. There is nothing more embarrassing than indiscriminate protection. I point out that a good burglar alarm would be cheaper to install and maintain.

So with goats. I dread selling them, except to established goat keepers. They are often wanted for curious reasons:

"I wish you'd sell me one of your goats. My garden is terribly overgrown, and the grass in the orchard's waist high."

I sometimes feel wickedly inclined to lend them one for the orchard! I say that it would be more practical to get a temporary gardener or a lawn-mower. And even in ideal conditions, one single goat would probably pine and die.

They are the most relative-conscious creatures I know. Great-great grandmothers, seventh cousins twice removed, will be accepted into the herd as a matter of course, once the leader has inspected and given consent. But try to introduce new blood and see where it gets you! Most probably you will have to send the newcomer back whence it came, or it would be battered to death.

I adopted a kid, Gazelle, and brought her up on the bottle from five days old. She lived with us in the house, played with the dogs and cats and exercised with the retrievers as she grew. At four months old I think she fully believed that she was a golden retriver. To compromise I called her the Golden Roat.

At that age I ventured to lead her amongst the other goats, who turned nasty from the word "go". Niall took one contemptuous sniff before urging the herd to battle.

Easing Gazelle into that herd took months of tactful persuasion. Even then she was only tolerated, and many a vicious nip of the ear or crashing bump mid-ribs was hers. Whenever I appeared with the dogs she would tear after us, only too glad to escape her solitary life in a growing herd who wanted none of her.

When at last she was in kid I let her have a stable to herself at night in case she should be hurt. I felt far from sanguine as to how her child would be received.

Sylvan, her daughter, was three days old when I put her in the sunshine with her mother. Niall and the others were some fields away.

Kids are the most photogenic creatures. I rushed into the house for my camera. When I went back I was alarmed to see

Niall, head lowered, walking menacingly towards mother and child. She was followed by eight suspicious goats, all prepared to become highly indignant.

If I shooed them away, or rushed Gazelle and the kid into a stable it might only make matters worse later. I decided to let events take their course, and watched.

After all, Niall knew what it was to be a mother, times over. Perhaps she would not punish at once, but wait until the baby Sylvan could make better use of her stilt-like legs.

Niall advanced solemnly and alone. The herd widened into a semicircle some distance away, waiting. She might have been a high priestess, performing some age-old rite. Certainly tradition must have explained her actions in the next moments.

The atmosphere was tense. Gazelle, still weak from a difficult birth, could not have run away; certainly she would not, leaving her precious one to the onslaughts of the leader.

Aloof, Niall ignored her, passing on to the soft white kid who stood, legs apart, surveying its new world in dazed wonder. Gazelle remained very still.

Niall nosed the kid gently. She inspected both ends of her. Then, astonishingly, she passed on to the mother, giving her a soft push in the neck.

Then, raising her head, Niall curled her top lip before crying: "Ble-eeer!"

At the signal the other goats came, in single file, to inspect the newcomer. One by one they lowered their heads, following the example of their leader in detail.

Soon Gazelle, unscathed, stood up in the centre of an admiring ring with the baby Sylvan beside her, more than pride of motherhood shining in her eyes.

From that moment she was one of them. She could share food and water with all. Because of the child she had given to the Dovey Herd, she would be protected by them for evermore. So it has proved.

I can think of one very practical reason for such odd behaviour. Sylvan was sired by the father of Niall's grandchildren. There was now a blood relationship. It could be that Niall merely had a change of heart, as well she might, when Sylvan stared back at her in all-trusting innocence. But, knowing the implacability of goats, I veer towards the first suggestion.

Although domestic goats are hardy, they need sound, dry cover available at all times from rain and worse. Where a horse will welcome natural cover of trees or protecting bushes, a goat will rush to its stable or shed as soon as the first spots of rain fall. The building can be kept open day and night, providing it is not draughty. Clean, dry bedding is another essential.

There is one fallacy I should like to explode about goats. They do *not* smell. At least, nanny-goats don't. I once made the same statement in the *Observer*, who had printed the couplet:

"The goat that reeks on yonder hill
Has grazed all day on chlorophyll."

I couldn't let such erroneous statement, even in quotation form, pass without protest.

Billy-goats can reek to high heaven in the mating season, which is from November until March. If allowed to run on free range their scent, which is worn only in the head, is much less pungent. Nannies who hobnob with the billy can pick up that tweedy aroma, to a lesser degree. If allowed to lie about in dirty stables they, or any other animal, will smell. So should I!

To "play the giddy goat" is a most apt allusion. When a cold, sunny morning, or the light of a full moon *gets* them, their antics are extraordinary.

They will waltz round on hind legs for incredible periods before lurching forward to crash heads or horns with another. Then ten steps backwards, to gain impetus for further and more violent onslaught, is a wonderfully popular move.

They leap against an eight-foot wall, almost at its apex, touching it with hind legs as a spring board.

Or four, leaning full weight against each others' ribs, push against another four from the opposite direction.

Why not? After all some of us have our odd relaxations. Golf, football, tennis, even bridge players must look awfully queer to goats.

I have watched a goat patiently teaching a retriever puppy to butt, pushing head to head. The puppy loves it, for a time. When it is more mature such enthusiasm wanes, probably because it has learnt who had the harder head.

Events took a different course when I adopted Jane the lamb. Her mother died when she was three days old and the shepherd, swinging her by the hind legs, asked in passing: "I suppose you don't want her?"

I didn't, but I had her. She was like a large catkin. The only strong thing about her were dainty, polished hoofs.

At first a doll's bottle proved easier to hold than a fountain-pen filler although the latter would have provided an ample meal for her puny needs.

It seemed unlikely that anything so small and helpless could thrive by human effort. Diluted goats' milk was varied by thin cornflour or weak Bengers Food. A few sips every hour, day and night, were effectual.

She decided to live. She did that mostly on laps, hot water bottles or by a log fire. The retrievers helped, but soon even Nada's warm affection could not withstand those ivory feet pommelling where they hurt most. Nada then passed her on to Bracken. Bracken soon transferred her to her own daughter, Sheena.

Snip lifted a lip in disdain—I like to think it was only that. On arrival in Wales her terrier fun with sheep had been deflected by corporal punishment. Above all things, Snip hated punishment, although it cured her evil ways. She regarded Jane as the one creature whom she must never look at. Difficult! Jane was everywhere.

When at last Jane bounded on to Snip for joyful exploration, Snip forgot to bite or snarl. She tore into a corner, waiting for the worst.

I made a great fuss of Snip, explaining that Jane was the naughty one but was too small to be punished. I put them both on the sofa on either side of me, hoping for reconciliation on Snip's part. She went rigid and shut her eyes. "Take it away," said her averted head.

It was a tricky situation because Jane must live in the house for weeks yet. She would be far from safe with the goats.

The cats solved the problem. Cats usually do. The beautiful black and white Panda, noted for her nervous disposition, took to Jane in a big way. She met her by accident one evening in the kitchen and purred like mad. She had no maternal instinct, but something about that lamb stirred her.

Up went Panda's bushy tail as Jane tottered to her. They rubbed noses, Jane skipped and Panda did one of her rolls to show her pure white undercarriage.

Snip, who knew that feeding time was near, stood expectantly in the doorway. Her expression, when she saw Panda and Jane playing amiably, was nothing short of comical. She twisted her head one way and then the other.

Just then the tabby Michael came in, arched his back and spat; not at Panda, whom he tolerated on all occasions. That must have decided Snip.

Who was Michael anyway? Spitting at the lamb like that. Didn't the fool know that if you as much as *looked* at sheep there were vile things in store? So Snip ran at Michael, who cursed and jumped on a table.

I chose that moment to intervene. Having Jane's bottle ready, I showed it to her. It brought forth the usual heart-rending cry: "Mee-me-ee!"

I offered the bottle to Michael first. Snip barked furiously. Then I gave it to Jane, and Snip approved. She licked the surplus milk from Jane's chin and liked the taste. I gave Snip the last few drops.

Then I put Jane out of doors—she was house-trained by Nada, who insists on cleanliness amongst the young—and Snip went with her. They came back together and sat by the fire, friends for life.

Strangely, when Jane was five weeks old she took the goats by storm. Thinking that she would be done to pulp, I ran out to save her. There was no need for alarm. Niall was laughing like anything. Her top lip curling, the old goat shook with mirth. So the other goats tittered, too.

Jane's skipping and butting they took in good part, although she was not allowed near udders. Correction took a mild form.

But it was weeks before they accepted her in the stable at night. This was, I thought, decidedly odd. Jane did not snore; the goats did. Could it be that she did not pull her orchestral weight? Whatever the reason, at nightfall she was gently but firmly pushed outside.

It didn't matter in the least, because Jane preferred to sleep with the dogs. It was not long before she came down to the village shop with the gang, on a collar and lead.

As spring mellowed into summer Jane gradually merged into the herd. By nightfall they were all so replete that no goat seemed to notice that Jane had a personality all her own. She slept with them, keeping her superiority complex to herself. But whenever the dogs appeared there was, and still is, a grand reunion.

Because Jane and Sylvan were babies at the same time, they often came for an evening walk with the dogs. Gazelle usually came too, to keep an eye on her daughter. Sylvan would bounce away from her to prance and leap with the lamb. Their antics even enchanted the cats, who followed in line at a discreet distance.

Along narrow, twisting paths we wove through the forest to the melody of homing birds. Seagulls, owls and the cuckoo in full voice were no more incongruous together than my motley crew.

More than once on such a walk I have glanced back at them, laughing at the memory of a similar trek in very different circumstances. It would seem that I am always followed by animals in the country.

It was in Tanganyika and an area which boasted more wild game than in any other part of Africa. I had been in that country only ten days and knew only that the next small settlement was over a hundred miles away.

I decided to take an afternoon stroll to the boma—a group of government offices, which included the post office—returning, as I thought, by the same sandy road.

But I must have walked for nearly a mile when a suspicion began to grow. Could there have been forked roads meeting at the boma? Certainly the undergrowth seemed deeper than I had known it, and where was the sea?

Just then a startling scream broke in on my thoughts. It sounded exactly like a pig being killed. About to retrace my steps, I turned to see a long-armed monster walking stealthily after me.

My knowledge of local fauna then was slight. I had no idea whether I was being followed by a gorilla, a chimpanzee, baboon or a species unknown, possibly an orang-outang.

I walked on a few paces to collect my thoughts, then glanced back. The monster was followed by several of its kind.

Instinctively I began to run. It was 110° in the shade and my heel was developing a blister. I thought that absolute quietness meant that I was no longer being followed. A desperate glance over my shoulder told me how wrong I was.

From an amble they had broken into a lope and, as my steps quickened, so did theirs. It would soon become a flat race, which I had no hope of winning.

Then common sense and exhaustion pulled me up. I was doing the worst possible thing by running on. There was only one course left to me. I should have tried it sooner—attack.

Waving a large sun hat, I cried: "Shoo!" The result was immediate. They all sat down on their heels; quite a ridiculous sight. The largest of them pressed his knuckles into sand, then started forward again. I repeated the heartfelt cry. It was effective.

With one accord, they slunk off into the bushes and, at last, I moved slowly on. But not far.

The country was growing more desolate. I must have taken the wrong path. To rectify the mistake I must pass back through the *gorillas*, as I mentally termed them.

Should I return sauntering nonchalantly, hurry, or walk with all the dignity I could muster? I decided on an impressive gait.

When I reached the spot where I had last seen them there was not a sound or movement.

Left, right; left, right. I swung along with military precision, not deigning—or daring—to glance backwards.

I lost count of time and distance in my dire need to keep up appearances. Once I heard a scream, unpleasantly near, followed by silence.

Fear changed my movements to a sort of goose step. So, head erect, I carried on like that until the boma appeared in the distance.

I was still moving very carefully indeed when I grew aware that, in front of the boma, three European doctors were doubled up with laughter. They must be laughing at me, since no one could be following on such a deserted road. I looked back.

Behind me, quite solemnly following and less than twenty yards away, were seven baboons. Left, right; left, right; one leg thrust forward, then the other. Arms swinging and heads as erect as they could be.

It was too much. I sat down on a tuft of white grass and, head in hands, laughed and laughed, mainly with relief. Behind me two brave baboons were doing just that: sitting down, heads in hands. The others had skulked off because the smell of mankind was getting too much for them.

The men's laughter also bore a modicum of relief. A native had related seeing the new mem-sahib walking alone in the wrong direction half an hour ago.

"Half an hour? Half a life ago, you mean." Then I asked them how the native knew that I was going in the *wrong* direction.

"My dear girl, there's not a building for twenty miles along there. You were heading straight for lion country. Another half mile and you'd have found the place infested with them."

The fact that they were about to race after me in the jeep was poor consolation to my shattered nerves. They would hardly have reached me in time had it not been for my other peculiar encounter.

I soon grew to appreciate the maxim: if you *see* dangerous game in Africa, it's too late. The visible usually proves harmless unless provoked to sudden fear or anger. The invisible is safer in that state, unless you are a seasoned game hunter.

So when my innocuous friends follow me I have reason to be grateful for our indigenous safety.

Because goats just will not keep to static numbers I registered them. Now it would be difficult to picture Pant Glas without the Dovey Herd. The white thread, weaving its way through spring verdure or across the russet carpet of autumn, seems as integral as the slopes on which they graze the year round.

If a possible enemy appears, in the form of a shepherd's dog or a tousled mongrel who fancies dalliance with the golden dogs, the goats form an immediate circle. The circle moves slowly towards the stranger. In the centre is Jane, now a full-grown sheep.

The circle breaks into an arc. Jane still in the middle. Then, boldly, she steps forward. Advancing upon the enemy, sometimes only a breath away, Jane stamps her feet. Usually this is effective.

But should the unbidden one snap or bark, the goats lower their heads, ready for battle. On such rare occasions they do support Jane.

If real trouble seems likely, then the horses join in. Whether this is at a signal from Niall, or because of their own assessment of a situation, I'm not sure. A mild canter from the heavy brigade puts most trespassers to flight.

Animals living freely together, as they do here, have a wonderful partisanship. They seem to move in separate groups, grazing different areas, impervious to the other species around.

But let there be one movement likely to affect all or any of them, then with one converging action they are together. This is especially so at feeding times, or when I walk among them.

It would seem that hearing and eyesight do not account for the full extent of their peculiar knowledge. Habit, instinct, the sense of smell and memory all play a part. But I believe that each of them has a middle eye which, unseen by us, sees all.

If I put a suitcase by the Land-Rover it isn't unreasonable that noses and beaks appear suddenly to inspect. But if, as has happened more than once, I walk briskly from the cottage, put my case in the vehicle and drive a quarter of a mile to the lower gate, to find the majority hovering there, *is* that coincidence?

I prefer to call it the *middle eye*, which forms such sound knowledge and uncanny action.

Chapter Five

"**D**o you keep poultry?"

For nearly four years the answer was: "No." I had been told that they would do very well at Pant Glas; plenty of free range. Or, if I really wanted to make it pay, there was nothing like *battery*.

The very word makes me shudder. If poultry couldn't pay *and* have a happy, natural life with me I wasn't interested. It did seem foolish to add yet another variety of livestock to the premises unless it did pay.

At last I decided to try out a few, so contacted a poultry breeder, asking inane questions. Could he tell me what equipment I should need to keep about half a dozen hens? I explained that I knew nothing about them—a fact he must have gleaned by then. He could bring them to me the following evening or at the end of that week.

Having made up my mind to try the perilous adventure I just couldn't wait to see them.

He advised me to prepare nothing elaborate, and the next evening arrived with five hens and one cock. They were Rhode Islands crossed Light Sussex.

The fodder room would do, he said, helping me to fix poles across it for roosting. It seemed frightfully inadequate to me, but at least it would be cosy and fox-proof. We found orange boxes for nesting and, looking round, he remarked that they should do well up here. Then from his van he brought out six birds who spluttered and scurried into their new quarters.

"The cock hasn't had much freedom and he's young. The pullets should be laying within three weeks. Whatever you do, leave them shut in for at least three days."

I paid him five pounds ten shillings, thanked him and he left.

I was now a poultry keeper. The knowledge gave me an absurd thrill.

Knowing that they were safely housed, the obvious thing to do was to leave them alone until morning. I walked away—a few steps. Then I walked back again. They might just appreciate a word.

I opened the door a few inches. "Good night!" I said softly. "I hope you'll like it here."

Then I left them to sort out their wings, feet, sleeping-quarters and new matrimonial affairs.

I followed instructions closely, for a time. Feeding and watering in the shed seemed a mean arrangement, especially as glorious spring weather had begun. So on their second morning I ventured to suggest:

"Would you care to come for a short walk?"

Would they! Out they came, to flap red wings in radiant sunshine. There was no need for me to direct them. The cock spread his gorgeous feathers and green shaded wings, said something by way of command to his females, who followed dutifully.

Mrs. Henrietta, Mrs. Henry Wood, Caroline, Fanny and Peggy strutted in the wake of—Archibald, who most wisely set his route by a wire fence. This led them to the knoll and luscious freedom.

They looked so serious as they strutted by. Their names positively shouted themselves to me as they passed.

Mrs. Henrietta was obviously the head of the harem. Mrs. Henry Wood looked about her with interest; she wore rather a literary air, I fancied. Caroline was an unknown quantity; she still is. Fanny vaguely reminded me of someone. Peggy — warm, kind Peggy — was just that.

Archibald? It was my father's name, and no one ever queried his command. He was majestic in a military manner and had — a presence. He dealt ably with most situations. The cock also had a decided personality.

The birds neither got lost nor flew away. They wisely followed Archibald's strut, uphill, downhill then to the brook to drink and look for things. They appeared to have accepted me.

We soon became firm friends. I shall never forget the thrill of hearing Archibald's first "Ah-doodle-oodle-oo", as he stood leg-deep in violets and primroses on a green bank by the barn. It was a sound of absolute acceptance and appreciation.

The very next day I gathered three eggs. I telephoned the breeder who was astonished, because the pullets were only just five months old.

Within exactly two months to the day of their arrival I had gained from my new family one hundred and ninety eggs and twenty-one chickens. The latter were proudly owned by Mrs. Henrietta and Peggy. All survived and are grown to full estate, most of the chickens being pullets, now in full lay.

I had gained much else as well. The discovery that poultry are affectionate, intelligent and friendly came as a surprise. For instance, whenever I called Archibald by name the dear thing ran to me eagerly, and not because of odd titbits. I kept to strict feeding times. With an "Ah-doodle-oodle-oo" he spread his wings for my special benefit. We sang "oodle-doo" duets, which I admit would have looked and sounded queer had anyone called on us suddenly.

One day, when Archibald was in his prime, and knew himself to be indispensable, a visiting puppy gave chase. Although I was soon there to defend him he had been driven into water. He caught a chill and died.

He had been with me only a few months but was then the father of twenty-one yellow chickens. I felt his loss deeply. So did poor Henrietta, who had been his devoted chief wife. She rushed about crying: "Whuk-di-di-di-di-di-di-dear" all day long. It was a pathetic little sound.

I could bear her grief, because I shared it, only for a few hours. Then I saddled up the cob, rode through the forest and called on Mrs. Jones.

There is always a kind Mrs. Jones in Wales. This one is particularly so. Her eyes filled with tears. She, too, had been genuinely fond of Archibald.

I asked if she would sell me one of her cockerels. She wanted to give him to me. We argued. I forget who won. That evening the magnificent Plymouth Rock took up residence at Pant Glas.

Pewter, the only possible name for him, had a scarlet crest and a fine physique.

Henrietta, loyal Henrietta, would have none of him. She turned aside, pecking listlessly. The fickle Caroline rolled an eye in his direction and sidled towards him, but little Fanny already stood demurely beside him.

Pewter, astounded at his new freedom—he was to have been killed shortly—took to his new family and sleeping-quarters in dazed content.

The next morning when Henrietta walked up my arm to my shoulder—they frequently do that—I could see that she was still upset.

"Never mind, darling. We shall get used to it in time." I didn't believe my statement any more than she did. I fed her by hand. But she had her children to console her; that was something.

It was Fanny who intrigued me. Although a regular layer, she was undersized and had an apologetic tail. Spinsterish, I thought, even when she edged up to Pewter. She stayed beside him all day, seeing him through his first bewilderment at so much freedom. When he strayed too far, Fanny led him back. By evening she was self-appointed mistress of the harem. She has remained so ever since.

Fanny slept beneath Pewter's wing that night, utterly content. But, after Archibald, I wondered if he were rather dull, although I couldn't deny his good looks.

Not one sound did he make. I had brought him here to remedy the harrowing loss of the "oodle-doodle-doo". Our home was suddenly like a desert.

Pewter seemed oblivious to Fanny, unless she was absent for a few minutes. Then he would give a perky look round and she trotted dutifully back to him. It was like watching a silent film.

The beautiful Mrs. Henry Wood, Caroline and the others didn't stand a chance beside Fanny. Through sheer, dull persistence, she was never ousted from his side.

I spoke to him; he didn't answer. He remained a grey, massive bird of distinctive appearance.

Then, one morning when the mountains were amethyst in heather, Henrietta raised her head and listened joyfully. So did I.

"Ah-doodle-ah-doodle-ah-doodle-oodle-oo!"

Pewter, King, was announcing the fact.

He flapped his wings, tried his magnificent voice again, and his wives, including Henrietta, rushed to pay him homage.

Pant Glas quickened its lovely melodies. The brook bubbled and splashed. Blue-tits, yellow hammers, blackbirds and many others sang—*sang*. Over the bogland curlews called, and high above the Plinlimmon range buzzards mewed—rather like rusty hinges.

Can one so mourn a cock, for two and a half weeks, to the exclusion of sounds such as those? Because, like Henrietta, I had been listening for a crow which never came, all other sounds had faded. It had been like living with a clock for months before suddenly hearing its tick.

As Pewter tried out his voice at frequent intervals, I inspected the chickens. Some were losing their yellow charm. They were strong and promised well. One was darker than the others. In fact, he was so nearly . . .

I went closer. There were bottle-green streaks already in his wings. I called him Nearly; the name suited him then.

Six weeks later I followed Nearly across the grass, watching his thrusting manner and the imperious tilt of his head. I whispered:

"I think you might become Archibald the Second. You are *his* son."

The fact registered not at all with Nearly. He was engrossed with the problem of a worm—already well in the beak of a larger chap than he. Without hesitation, he dealt with the matter. There was no flurry; just firm insistence that the worm should go down *his* throat. It did.

"Good for you—Archibald!"

Now Archibald the Second, once named Nearly, reigns over one half of the poultry family; Pewter over the other half. It is a most happy arrangement. I suspect that Pewter decides who shall have who, or they might draw lots during the night.

I was compelled to harden my heart over the few remaining cockerels, grown to full size at Christmas. Those for whom I couldn't find good homes had known wonderful happiness and freedom in their shorter lives.

It was such a pleasure to make the acquaintance of a retailer who sells eggs from free-range hens only. He sells what he terms "happy eggs", including mine.

It is interesting to note that these happy hens produce slightly larger, certainly better quality eggs, and just as many of them, as those poor creatures who live in perpetual captivity, to the glare of false lighting, and having no fun at all.

My animals are extremely fond of music. The poultry are no exception. Often on a sunny day, when the B.B.C. obliges, I take the radio on to the terrace.

Strauss is most popular with the goats and horses. They like dreamy melodies. The hens, their heads perked on one side, come a little nearer, then nearer still.

A good marching tune brings them all to the gate, and the goats waggle their beards in approval.

Mendelssohn's *Spring Song* brings Pewter and his shadow, Fanny, hurrying forward, obviously hanging on to every note. Fanny does a little skip, peculiar to her. A late-comer or so come at the run, looking quite stupid with their heads poked forward and necks elongated.

Jane, chewing the cud, lies sublimely content among a welter of hoofs, feet and claws, her head slightly swaying to the music. Does she dream of long evenings spent with dogs and cats before a log fire, or of flocks on mountains? If the latter, she shows no desire to join them. She is a very happy sheep and often smiles as she chews.

The music ends and an announcer's voice is heard. They all wander off in pairs, in groups or singly, nibbling or pecking as they go to other entertainment.

The dogs watch me. The cats watch no one, but see all. "Surely she won't go back to the writing-room yet?" their expressions say. It was my intention. But the air of expectancy is too much. We shall have to compromise.

"Very well—just half an hour."

All bedlam is let loose. The retrievers and Snip rush back and forth until the gate is opened. All give tongue. A second gate a few yards ahead leads to paradise. They are eager for it.

Click and open: away they're gone. Down through the forest and up again; up, up, up. Down they tear to the path I stroll along, followed by four cats.

Chita, because she is Siamese, follows to heel—a most satisfactory "dog". Her kitten, Lissa, skips alongside, stopping now and then to look through her own hind legs to see if China is coming. He is, and at a remarkable gallop.

China is pure white, and of near Siamese extraction. He is large at nearly two years old and likely to grow more.

Michael, aged fifteen years, is not to be outdone. He is nearly twice China's size and weight and, if his back is somewhat stiffer, he hates anyone to notice the fact. His lope brings him level with the others. Soon he stays behind to sharpen his claws on a tree. "There's no need to hurry. I've done all this before, many times." That's what his slightly bored expression says to me. He sits down and waits for the return trek.

The dogs are eager to go and eager to come back. Whether they rush about, or walk sedately to heel, according to temperament, no direction is a bad one.

When I gather firewood they love to help. Nada grasps a stout branch in the middle, her daughter and granddaughter taking up positions on either side. Heads high, the golden trio bring their offering to me, their plumes waving elegantly.

This is a favourite game on the beach. Wonderful swimmers, they love nothing better than to retrieve wood floating beyond high waves. Sometimes they and the wood disappear, only to emerge in glistening triumph, heading for the shore. Their team-spirit is remarkable, fostered by Nada's patient teaching of the young.

Not only has she trained her two litters, nineteen puppies in all, but she has taken over Bracken's children at the appropriate time. Anything young comes under Nada's care, including lambs and kids who are bottle reared. All are house-trained by Nada. Chita sees to the training of her own children, for she, too, has the hall-mark of an aristocratic parent.

As soon as a puppy has passed the tumbling stage, Nada

68

presents a stick. The puppy thinks this great fun, sits and chews one end; but not for long. It is prodded into action and made to grasp the stick in the right place, and eventually, facing the right direction. Lack of concentration is corrected in a flash.

Born to love water, Nada knows that a nervous puppy shouldn't be hurried. Usually retrivers are five months old before she gives them serious instruction. Then she coaxes, never forces, them from shallow water to their first short swim. When all fear has gone and breathing comes easily, usually at the second lesson, she takes them for a *real* swim.

It's a grand sight to see half a dozen of them negotiating a river or lake with the ease of swans.

The moment a pupil loses confidence, treading water anxiously, Nada is beside it, encouraging for all she's worth.

Then comes the proud moment when she returns with them, all shaking water over me. Her deep brown eyes are raised to mine. She might well be saying: "There you are. It's a proper dog now."

It is Niall who teaches the young goats what to eat, where to graze and when.

But with the poultry, most oddly, it is Fanny who takes all such duties upon herself. At over a year old she bustles about, still minus tail, putting everyone right. She is never far from Pewter, who hovers like a heavy-weight golf champion, his old-fashioned *plus fours* bearing strange contrast to his brilliantly scarlet crest.

Fanny it is who sees that the other hens and pullets lay where they should. At least, she tries to. A hen, old enough to know better, discovered nesting in the hay, drives Fanny into a terrible state. She screeches and flaps her wings, uttering: "Terk-uk-uk-uk, terk-uk-uk-uk", with the persistence of an outraged housewife whose children have upset ink on the carpet.

If Pewter is too resigned to such domestic trivialities, Archibald the Second comes to see what he can do about it.

By now the family is divided into two sections: Archie-birds and Pewter-birds. Pewter has a few more wives than Archibald, which is as it should be. Archibald has agility; Pewter all the *aplomb* due to a king.

When Fanny has recourse to Archibald—a measure she often adopts—he is delighted. Willingly he singles out a hen, with a "Whee-whee-whee-werk-we", which means that the culprit is where "she didn't oughter be". If one of his own wives errs he gives a special nip; if one of Pewter's, he shoos and leaves it at that.

Then, deluded by a bright eye, he returns to Fanny's side to gather, at least, some gratitude. "Wherk!" is her unkind response. She runs to Pewter, muttering under his wing. Whatever vile interpretation she gives we shall never know, for certain.

Pewter does what any man must do in such circumstances: he goes for Archibald with a flurry of grey wings and mighty weight. No harm is done, but a code of ethics is re-established for at least another day. And Fanny goes on pecking by his side.

I have just solved a mystery: how do twenty hens lay thirty-six eggs in one day? The tabby Michael told me, with a yawn. That artful old cat, whom I thought was watching for mice in the hay, had been sitting on seventeen eggs. I don't know for how long, but they tasted fine.

The initial introduction of dogs and cats to poultry wasn't as difficult as I had anticipated. Snip, who is inclined to attack first and to think afterwards, was first to be taken out on a lead to say "how do you do".

Her unusual form of restriction warned her that something was "up". It was indeed, very up. So were her hackles, but only for a moment or so. My use of her name in three distinct notes, on a rising scale, bore unspoken threat of a spanking.

She sniffed the earth, her eyes remaining in the direction of those delicious feathers. Hundreds and thousands of feathers to scatter in the air!

Just then a hen, looking for something she couldn't find immediately, threw up soil with her feet. It landed in Snip's face—the ultimate affront!

Snip gave an explosive bark. I growled at her. Beset by enemies, she tugged for the home gate. Not wanting to make bad blood on either side, I took her back. Repeating the visits twice daily, having given the retrievers similar treatment, seemed to be a success with Snip.

Nada and Sheena were good from the start. Sheena's mother, Bracken, was inclined to be "bouncey". When all three were duly reliable I let Snip join us, without a lead, when the poultry was fed.

All went well, for a time. Snip behaved like a choir boy in white surplice, and looked rather like one. Then, suddenly, she spotted the very hen who had thrown dirt in her face.

"As for *you* . . ." it sounded like. I didn't stay to hear the rest.

In seconds calm was restored and no harm done. For a week Snip stood on the safe side of the gate watching the retrievers moving about freely with me among the birds. She was not amused.

For the same reason her walks were restricted to the forest, which she adores. But it isn't the same as being on one's own land. After all, she had found the place, hadn't she? If it hadn't been for her, urging Nada and Bracken to make a commotion one hot June day, where should we all be now? And where would those beastly chickens be, eh? In somebody's battery. The best place for them, too!

I saw such thoughts written on her face as she peered through the gate, but I hardened my heart. Everyone must live peacefully with everyone else here, or not at all. I had told Snip so many times. Despite terrier urges, the lesson was due to sink in.

At last one morning I opened the gate, taking four dogs with me to the chickens. I adopted an attitude which I did not altogether feel to be justified: naturally all dogs would ignore the sudden onrush of birds as I let them into the sunlight.

And they did. Snip has never again taken evil interest in poultry. Now they can flurry over her back or "Wherk" near her face, without such diversion swaying her from her course.

But let any visiting dog so much as look at a hen, then Snip goes into prompt and fierce attack of the dog. She is a fanatical protectress of us all.

Any day now new beaks will burst the shells so carefully guarded by Caroline, Rose and Plush. Mrs. Henrietta has gone into a trance and is about to sit perfectly still for three weeks. Her eyes are glazed with expectancy.

Little Fanny plods along beside Pewter. *Sit*—for three

weeks? Not she. The fact that she has never yet gone broody seems remarkable for such a good layer and housewife. Or is it so strange? She has the two males completely under her rule.

"Wherk-uk-uk!"

"Yes, my girl. And who's doing the 'werk', eh? Not you, that is a fact."

Her unblinking stare denies all knowledge of my meaning. She perks her head swiftly, then scurries forward, urging Archibald to follow. He does so with the best of intentions. Pewter can't come just now; he's busy with an obstinate tuft of grass.

Another pullet laying in the hay? Dear, innocent Archibald! Nothing of the sort.

Once in the dutch barn Fanny peeps round the corner to see if Pewter is still safely engaged. He is. "Cluk-cluk." Her head darts down and—well, *really*!

Her appalled shriek brings Pewter galloping to the rescue. He and Archibald stand beak to beak until Pewter, with a frightening wing flap puts the other to flight. It would be quite useless for poor Archibald to explain that he only meant to help. That when Fanny called him he had no idea . . .

And Fanny trots along in Pewter's wake, peck-pecking as she goes; the dutiful, adoring wife. The hussy!

"Yes, I keep poultry," I tell casual inquirers. I don't add that I wouldn't be without them for a king's ransom; that they have opened up a new world of rich, perpetual entertainment.

Chapter Six

As soon as the goats had approved Pant Glas and accepted me I knew that something was missing.

For the first time in twenty years Ballygiblin's saddle might have been carved in stone, a cold monument. Morose thoughts were no fit tribute to such a friend. I must find a horse at once, worthy of that saddle and its happy memories.

This is not thoroughbred country. Its very contours demand staying power, but of the slow and sure type.

My thoughts dallied with that mystifying term, often seen in advertisements: "The perfect *confidential* cob." Having been a confidential secretary for too long, it was difficult to dissociate such a quality from a shorthand notebook.

I admit to a certain lack of enthusiasm at such a prospect. Gone were the days when silken movement would carry me, at speed, over fields, ditches, fences; when fine skill lay with the mount rather than with the rider. "*Can* you do it, boy?" The next instant, with a flourish of tail, the unspoken reply: "I have," and that proud lift of the head as further obstacles were assessed.

I pictured myself now trundling round exquisite countryside —up, up and sometimes down—above the feathered legs of some light-weight cart-horse. Better that than no horse.

In such a mood I visited the Llanarth Stud, where preconceived notions were swept aside. A galaxy of Palamino cobs cantered to see—who now? Their golden manes and tails brought sunshine with them.

After affectionate nosings and greetings they went back to their own affairs. There was not an awkward movement among them.

Inspection of the mares and foals, the stallions and of various geldings confirmed my growing respect for the pure bred Welsh cob. There was nothing unwieldy or cumbersome about them, no dinner-plate feet, dishing action or hairy legs.

I was told that Llanarth Siriol, half-brother to the famous champion, Llanarth Braint, might suit me. He was nine years old and greatly loved. I was taken to a field where a dozen or more cobs grazed. They moved towards us. Farther away a dark bay lifted his head. He stood, listening. Then, without hesitation, he made up for lost time; a real warrior's horse.

I noticed his powerful shoulders, proud head carriage, excellent quarters and, although I tried to ignore it, the white star. Strangely, with the exception of a grey pony, I've always had a bay horse with a star on the forehead. The star was smaller but identical in shape to Ballygiblin's.

One should not choose a horse by colour or markings, I knew. But when I saw the large eyes, slightly triangular, and the amused question which lay in them: "Who—*me?*"—I hoped sincerely that this was Llanarth Siriol.

"This is Llanarth Siriol."

He gave me a wholesome shove with his nose when I touched the white star. I was told of his affectionate disposition, how he had been sold to a hunting family but returned to his breeders through eventual circumstances. I was assured of his patent safety qualities. Possibly I looked nervous; I was—at his price.

Another shove in my back sealed the deal: "Go on—you'll manage it." If that's what he said, he was right. His purchase price has since proved cheap indeed.

Two days later I met Siriol in Aberystwyth and rode him nine miles home. He had not been ridden for a year but behaved remarkably well.

It soon became clear that he was not traffic-shy. When a train thundered by in a cloud of steam at Bow Street, I wondered for one moment if he might be slightly "nappy". That term means: "No, most certainly not", and going into reverse gear, side-stepping and generally playing the fool.

He was not nappy. He responded to the aids—leg pressure and hands telling him firmly what was wanted—admirably.

Then we reached Pant Glas. As I leaned over his neck to open the gate he let out a neigh. The sound was not unlike a liner coming into dock. He dismissed the steep rise in one swift gallop, until I said that we must arrive home cool and at the walk.

His head turned right and left in obvious inspection. Constantly he welcomed himself home with his terrific call. "Here I come—Llanarth Siriol!" It began as a bass song, ending in tenor key.

I've never known a horse who chattered so much and who took such profound interest in everything and everyone.

The goats met us at the stables. Niall, Bambi and Belinda lowered their heads. Niall, keeping hers lowered, came forward to discover more. I dismounted and led Siriol to her.

It was an anxious moment because Siriol could have disposed of the goats if he chose.

They smelt noses. Siriol blew hot air over Niall who, raising her top lip, laughed like anything. Her horned daughters then joined in close inspection while I unsaddled.

After much petting and one-sided conversation, I added: "It's all yours, Siriol. I think the goats will show you round."

That was just what they did. Waiting until Siriol had thundered up and across several fields to get his bearings, the trio joined him at more leisurely pace. By then he knew that he was going to be quite glad of their company.

I had been assured that, although a good mixer, Siriol would not be miserable on his own. He was a very *personal* horse.

I found this to be so, especially at milking time. He never failed to lean over the stable door and run his muzzle over the back of whichever goat was being milked. If the "swish-swish" of milk were halted for any reason, Siriol would apply light pressure of teeth to the goat's rump, sometimes with disastrous results. Rather than cut off his social activities by shutting the top half of the door, I became a dexterous milker.

Belinda adored him from the beginning. She is still often to be seen rubbing her horns on Siriol's chin, or standing underneath him. Although he exceeds fifteen hands, she has to leave her horns outside. They never hurt each other. I have seen him peep through his forelegs to see if she is still there.

Possibly colour affinity draws them, for Belinda is the only brown goat on the premises. Her drooping ears, bequeathed by an Anglo-Nubian father, give her special attraction. Siriol thinks so, too.

That first winter I grazed twenty sheep for a local farmer.

They thrived on the good grass, as Siriol did in their company. He moved about with them and was often to be found lying down, sheep and goats nibbling round him.

Once he overslept, waking to find a deserted field. There was a frightful hullabaloo as he went galloping in all wrong directions, until he went through the woods to the lower fields and found them.

He didn't disappoint me under the saddle. Looking exactly like a warrior's charger, he is light in action and easily managed. He walks out well and has a tremendous gallop. He dearly loves a solid jump and pulls to get at it, negotiating it with ease and safety.

Without tremor I can ride him on a narrow path with a frightening drop below, knowing that if anything startled him he would not shy in the wrong direction. He has great common sense, and staying power.

In fact I have found that Siriol is not a paragon; he is merely a typical Welsh cob. He lives out, winter and summer, from choice; the stable door is always open to him. He can be left in freedom and unridden for months, giving not a whit of trouble when saddled up again.

I was warned by horse owners—not to feed him. I have been warned by cat owners not to feed cats, or they won't kill mice. No one has ever warned me against eating, in case I don't write another word!

Why a naturally "good doer" should be deprived of moderate feeding I have never discovered. A horse living out in winter needs a little extra, not a great deal, for obvious reasons. Hay morning and night and a bowl of corn, in winter, is much sounder diet than wet, impoverished grass. So, too, in early spring when lush grass can play havoc; an armful of hay will stop a deal of trouble.

Too often one hears from the novice: "I daren't give my horse *corn*. I should never hold him."

A horse isn't a mechanical object into which you pour danger, in the form of good and natural food, extracting violent and dangerous action as a result.

An unfit animal is inclined to lack full energy. Would it be kinder to choose a fit animal we are able to control, rather than measure out starvation diet by our own incompetence?

As for properly fed cats not killing mice, mine would soon contradict that theory. They have milk, light breakfast and a good evening meal. The result is many, many slaughtered mice. When house mice diminish, the field mice are for it. They are rarely eaten. That is the criterion of a good mouse-killer. Once a cat eats mice for sustenance it is no longer sport. When satiated, the cat won't work, and with good reason. Mouse killing isn't work to well-kept cats; it's fun.

Siriol *cried* when the sheep left. His pitiful neigh sounded just like that, as he raced all over the place, looking for them.

I consoled myself with the knowledge that in three weeks' time six bullocks would arrive from the same source as the sheep. Those three weeks proved exhausting.

I saddled up five days a week, taking Siriol to the beach. There a three-mile stretch of hard sand made it pleasurable for us both. Sometimes we were escorted by a few children on ponies, their main delight being to jump the many solid groynes between Ynyslas and Borth. That is where I first discovered Siriol's fine jumping capacity, although at the time I deplored the heartless bravery of children.

Picturing knee-caps bashed against concrete posts, not comfortably wide apart, I need not have worried. Siriol sailed over. But he objected to pools of water. He was apt, at a flat gallop, to stop dead, apparently to admire his reflection. I cured this disconcerting habit eventually.

When the last groyne was safely negotiated I breathed with relief, only to find that those horrid children wanted to go back by the same route, instead of through country lanes. So we all jumped back again. It wasn't my idea of peaceful hacking!

Later, when he had rolled off brine and sand into home grass, Siriol began to look anguished. With what I call his "hands in pockets" expression, he mooched round, looking and calling for his lost sheep.

He grew slightly mollified at milking time. After that he took to kicking the kitchen door, for attention rather than for titbits.

By then I was writing and hoping not to be disturbed. In desperation I would take out the radio if the B.B.C. were providing light, preferably stirring, music. Siriol loves that. Unfortunately I'm one of those odd people who can't write novels to music. So, until the bullocks came, writing was confined to the small hours. It is a habit to which I've been addicted ever since.

On one still, summer night I was writing rather a hair-raising chapter. My heroine, full of premonition, was staring into the inky blackness—I knew exactly how she felt. It needed only a pair of eyes, glaring at her through black glass, to send her screaming mad. Not *screaming* mad; a heroine should remain poised, even when terrified. To send her . . . ?

For inspiration I looked at the inky glass, which in day-time reveals only the serenity of the forest and sea beyond. I wrote no more that night.

Immense, solemn eyes glared at me through black glass!

To say that my mouth went dry is an understatement. For seconds I felt *withered*; that could have been the word I had sought, but I didn't use it.

I must have stared for some moments at Siriol's long face and black forelock, flattened against the window, before sanity returned.

"S-Siriol, you shouldn't b-be here." I led him to the goats. That week the house was properly fenced and gated.

Six small bullocks arrived. Siriol loved them dearly. As the weather grew hotter he led them into the stable, where they all spent long summer days. At night I mucked out for a full hour before beginning to write.

In this green, sequestered valley they put on weight in no time. It was not long before they grew too heavy and inert for Siriol's liking. But he cantered round on his own, always returning to tell them where he'd been.

When the farmer came to collect his bullocks in the autumn he stared in pleased wonder. "They *must* have been happy here!" he exclaimed. Yes, I think they had been. They had grown enormously.

I felt rather like a mother, seeing her sons off to foreign shores, as I said good-bye to each bullock by name. In turn I rubbed them behind the ears and patted their necks. The farmer roared with laughter, saying that he'd have to keep them in the parlour from now on.

Siriol stood in a trance until the bullocks and their owner

were out of sight. Then he tore after them. I don't know what happened in the lower fields, but presently he galloped back, sounding like a train about to enter a tunnel. At intervals during the night and the next day he called for his friends — in vain.

I knew then that I must harden my heart. We faced winter. I couldn't afford the time or money to entertain the idea of a second horse. With moderate exercise, company of the goats, good food and as much shelter as he cared to take, Siriol's fate was not to be pitied.

I tried not to see him staring over a hedge when the faint clip-clop of hoofs sounded in the distant village. He was happy enough, I suppose.

One day in the spring I took him to the Aberystwyth Show, having entered him in the Cob Class. Although I had spent so many years with my own horses, this was my first attempt at showing. I did it purely for Siriol's entertainment; he loves a party.

From the time he entered the show ground he fully entered into the spirit of the occasion. Came the awful moment when, leading him by a new halter, I entered the ring.

Now, I'm quite capable on *top* of a horse, but put me beside one on a piece of rope, amid a confusion of horses, and I'm apt to get lost.

For those who show regularly it's child's play. They jiggle the halter and their horse stands immediately to attention, as if to the National Anthem, feet, head and tail just so.

When I do the same thing the effect on my horse is quite different. At once he engulfs me. Disentangled, I emerge on the off side, the halter still in my right hand, with the show specimen headed for the judge. A kind farmer shoves him in the chest and I am able to return to the near side, full of anxieties.

I heard someone admiring Siriol and remarking that when he ran he'd be likely to cause attention. That is what I feared. Desperately I looked round.

Heaven bless that well-known handler and breeder of Welsh ponies who came to my rescue then! I explained that I was not good at running. He offered to take the halter from me when the crucial moment arrived.

The judge, a famous cob fancier, scanned the line of exhibits. As he did so Siriol trod on my foot. I said: "Don't, darling," and pushed him back. The judge frowned, although he might not have been looking at me. Then he indicated that I should lead Siriol forward at the walk. I did so and was able to turn just in time to prevent his giving the judge an affectionate nudge in the stomach.

When I repeated the performance at the trot, six legs under my partial control seemed to develop centipede proportions. Siriol, thoroughly enjoying such inspection, swept me round at the appointed place, returning me to standing position.

The order was given to widen out and run the cobs round. My anguished glance showed me that my promised rescuer was deep in conversation. Siriol, tense with excitement, was ready to fling out with the best.

We were only half-way round when, head erect and eyes shining with excitement, he had outpaced me to the extremity of the halter. This was awkward because I was also being mowed down from the rear by another exhibit.

Never did words sound sweeter than: "All right. I'll run him for you."

Then I was able to watch my own cob cantering out in such exalted company. He did far better without my weight behind him and obviously enjoyed his competent handler, who had to leave me for the final judging, as he had his own ponies to get ready.

Standing still while others received red, blue, yellow and green rosettes on behalf of their winning cobs would be easy, if they didn't prolong it too much. I was asked to move to the left of the line.

A simple request? Not at all. I plaited Siriol's halter with that of the horse moving to the right. At the same time, in this unplanned game of "Oranges and Lemons", my hair became entangled with the button of a man's cuff, Siriol having dislodged my hat which he then stood on.

It was worth it. Siriol was so happy. He would be able to go home and dream of the horses he'd met that day. He is a great dreamer. He was dreaming when I was asked to move to the left again. We did that more successfully by taking an exaggerated semicircular route.

I consoled myself with the thought that at least we were not at the other end of the line, among the prize winners. They would have to hang around for another five hours and go in the Grand Parade. Soon I intended to slip away on Siriol, going home by lanes and mountains, instead of the main road.

A man came forward, handing me the red rosette. I pointed out his mistake. He looked startled, checked my number, stating: "I'm quite sure. This *is* Llanarth Siriol. The Judge sends his compliments and congratulates you on your courage in coming into the ring."

With twinkling eyes he left me to cope with thundering applause, Siriol, his rosette and my squashed hat. I was relieved that we didn't have to rush round again in a circle, for the whole affair had gone to Siriol's head.

Everyone patted him. He had a marvellous day and champed his way into the Grand Parade to music. We followed on the heels of the largest bull I've ever seen, who was quite un-moved by a marching tune. Happily the tempo changed just in time to prevent the bull and me making one.

We arrived home by horse-box in the evening, I with a splitting headache, Siriol with his rosette and trumpeting neigh which he hadn't indulged all day; I will say that for him.

During the day I had met the Judge. I thanked him for his verdict, apologizing for my lack of experience. I told him that I had never before shown a horse in hand.

"I could see that," he smiled. "But even your performance couldn't alter his conformation."

Weeks later the B.B.C. telephoned me, saying that they had heard I owned the best cob in Wales.

"*He* thinks so. But he isn't for sale."

That wasn't the point. They wanted him to appear on tele-vision, which he did.

Siriol and I spent a very pleasant week-end at Chepstow as guests of the B.B.C., appearing on a live programme one Sunday morning, in company with the great Foxhunter, the Coed Coch ponies and many other distinguished horses. Siriol had been selected as the outstanding and typical Welsh Cob.

After that I could no longer bear to see him staring at the distant sea for hours on end. He had lived for eighteen months with goats, sheep or bullocks, usually only with goats. Now he must have a companion.

Early in May I went again to Llanarth, where I bought a black mare, already served by Llanarth Braint. She was out of condition and had been unsound. She needed a kind home and, at least, was a proved brood mare.

Fortinus Bess arrived by horse-box two days later on a gloriously sunny morning. Siriol was lying in one of the top meadows when I went down to meet her.

Because Bess was unshod we made little sound coming up the hill. Siriol was still studying daisies.

Suddenly he raised his head, ears alert. Although some fifty yards away, he seemed in one swift movement to be at Bess's side, with the shrillest neigh of welcome Pant Glas has ever heard.

I removed her halter, saying to him: "This is Bess, Siriol. She's yours."

Indeed she was. They rubbed noses. Bess spoke to him in a sweet contralto tone, trotting to the middle of a field. Siriol danced round her, then prostrated himself at her feet. Up he rose and kissed her again, uttering what must have been her name. She replied softly, looking round at her new home with obvious approval.

This was expressed at last, when Siriol had rolled for the third time, by Bess joining him. She rolled and rolled, stood up, shook her full mane and looked ahead, as if to say: "Show me round the place!"

He did that. At first they walked, then trotted. He led her

to his favourite view of the wide landscape which ended with the sea.

That view is never the same from one hour to another. Even on a cloudless day the bog land colours shift and change in amazing sequence. Russet brown drifts into vermilion, ice blue and olive green for no apparent reason. It is rarely without a touch of coral. Sometimes towards the close of day it wears a white veil; a subtle means of reflecting later all the vivid beauty of a radiant sunset.

There they stood, side by side, for several minutes. Then for all the world it looked as if he whispered in her ear. Perhaps he said: "I'll tell you what—follow me."

Wheeling round, they galloped fast. Up the sloping fields to a level stretch, the extremity of the land they owned. They tore round there for a minute or so, then crashed down through the oak woods, across more flat turf until they reached the wooded knoll.

They were out of sight for moments before they appeared on the crest of the knoll, overlooking the Dovey estuary.

Soon they were back near the house for another roll, before trotting sedately down the path to the lower fields. Side by side, in every action they were together. They have been so ever since.

Bess proved a pleasant ride. Her endurance equalled Siriol's. Whenever a horse-loving friend came to stay with me, I willingly exchanged the typewriter for a saddle. After many a trek of twenty miles, with a break for a picnic lunch in the mountains, they returned cool and untired. I rode each in turn.

Bess's condition improved in a very short while. From a dusty black she soon glistened. Her action grew lighter, too, although by December I retired her until after her thrilling feat the next spring.

As a midwife Siriol excelled himself. I had never owned a mare before, so accepted much conflicting advice, which the horses disposed of when I tried to put it into practice.

Country folk told me that Bess would be far better foaling in the open. But many experienced horse owners shook their heads, muttering: "Risky!" Most people advised me to keep Siriol apart from Bess when the foal was due. That was as easy as dividing water.

All set to take no risks, I prepared the large stable, battening the sides and floor with plentiful straw. The foal was due on about the second of May. On the thirtieth of April all was ready. On that day Bess wore a dreamy expression, so I led her to the stable in the evening.

She ate some hay then demanded to be let out again. So I put Siriol in the stable. Bess refused to budge until I stopped his commotion by letting him out. Perhaps she would gradually take to the idea, coming indoors of her own accord.

At nine o'clock in the evening I went out, to see Bess following heavily after Siriol up to the favourite viewpoint. But she became quite skittish on level ground, so I thought that there was no need for concern that night.

Two hours later I went outside to see if all was well. The horses were not to be found. After much searching I heard Siriol's chuckle in the top field. So I went up with a torch.

In a far corner, as high as they could go, I heard them grazing and sniffing into the grass. It was strange that they didn't come to me when I called. Perhaps they were in a secretive mood.

Then Siriol chuckled again: "Huh-huh-huh!" Bess whinnied and a treble sound replied to her. I shone my torch on them and, to my consternation, counted twelve legs of equal length. Another horse must have broken in and joined them.

The circle of light encompassed three horses apparently grazing in supreme contentment. *Whose* was the third?

It was Siriol who, unable to contain himself any longer, ran to me, explaining. His voice rose in a squeak of excitement, as I stood beside the stranger saying: "No! I can't believe it. Are you really *mine*?"

"Ours," Siriol seemed to bellow, moving towards the house and urging me to do the same.

Bess nosed me gently before giving similar treatment to a perfect chestnut filly with a white blaze on her face. Bess turned to me again. I have never seen such adoring pride in a mother's eyes.

"So you are—*Pride*! Cardigan Pride!"

Yes, indeed she was, and terribly pleased to own me, judging from her wet kiss. Then she took several sophisticated steps towards her mother. I was too enchanted to move until Siriol bellowed me into action.

I fetched a bran mash and a bucket of tepid water for Bess, saving time by using the Land-Rover. Siriol, who had outpaced the vehicle, inspected both buckets. For once he didn't try to snatch a bite first. I travelled the last few yards on foot, he pushing me along gently with his nose. He shrieked with delight as Bess drank before disposing of the food.

Although dark, it was mild enough to leave the baby and her mother out. But the next evening, following Pride's tremendous first gallop, a storm broke. Rain lashed down as I went with a torch to find them. Bess was only too eager to follow me to the stable with Pride.

I wondered if Siriol might prove a nuisance until I shut the stable door. Not he. He stood at a discreet distance until I had closed the lower half of the door. Then he hung his head inside, guarding his adored ones. He was in that position the next morning until I let out the mare and filly.

Although Siriol was really Pride's uncle, I'm sure that such distant relationship didn't occur to him. They were the most united family I have known.

That spring there were kids and Jane, the lamb. Pride made full use of them all as playmates. If the kids looked like leading her into mischief, wandering too near a precipice drop of twenty feet, it was Siriol who tore after her, returning her safely to Bess.

At three days old she was taught by him to jump the brook, instead of calling after her mother who had gone ahead.

Having cleared the brook, Siriol turned to see Pride standing uncertainly on the far side. So he went back, nipped her rump gently and over they went together. They returned to do it again and again. Bess, a devoted mother, couldn't be bothered with such details. She left everything, except food, in Siriol's safe keeping.

When visitors called, Siriol would first trot along to see who they were. If he approved he went back for Pride, borrowing her for a few minutes from Bess. Then he would reappear, neighing and pushing Pride in front of him. He might, for all the world, have been saying: "See what we've got!"

He was delighted when everyone petted his darling. Although I had many good offers of purchase for her, it was not just her potential value as a brood mare which made me turn them down. I should never have faced Siriol again had I accepted one.

Little did I know then of a cloud which was spreading over Pant Glas, to deluge us in a storm of grief.

Chapter Seven

O<small>N</small> a late winter's morning, when the sun shone but the wind was cold, Pride galloped with her mother and uncle from the top fields to breakfast.

At nine and a half months her well-formed body and superb action were a joy to watch. With her usual cavorting but gentle grace, she was the embodiment of life and perfect happiness. Her chestnut coat glinted like burnished copper as she raced to my side, nuzzling my hand.

It was difficult to believe that a year ago such vigour and lively action, such visible ecstacy—a miracle of incarnation— had not existed.

There were workmen about. The cottage creaked and groaned under their efforts. I had heard that very old houses resent improvement; now I was beginning to believe it.

The men, collectively, seemed happy enough. They sang or whistled at work. The animals adapted themselves to the foreign whirl of activities as well as they could. At such times cats are the wisest creatures.

Panda, notorious for her nervous temperament, was the least disturbed. She hid in a loft until the last workman had left the premises at night. Then she appeared with a plaintive "miaow" for food and attention. She was clever enough to know if a man worked overtime, however silent he may be.

Not once did she make the mistake of showing herself a second before the final click of the gate.

When her loft was attacked she took refuge between chimney stacks or, in bad weather, in the forest. After the tragedy she stayed in the forest for a fortnight, only darting home for food late at night.

Chita, then a noisy kitten, wailed her Siamese tunes of happiness or despair from my shoulder most of the time.

On that particular day when the horses had finished breakfast, they galloped up the fields to take advantage of the sun which drenches Dovey meadow even when the wind is cold.

I thought of the time, at least two years ahead, when Pride would take her first real lessons. Already she was halter trained and the gentlest creature to lead. Expert care and tuition would be hers when she first worked under the saddle.

I had explained to a group of inquiring men just why a young horse could not be ridden. My shocked reply to the suggestion that if anyone rode her now they'd fall off, was: "It would kill her," going on to tell them how a young horse's body is formed and the long time it takes to reach maturity.

"Well, what about racehorses? They race them at two years old."

I agreed that two-year-old thoroughbreds were raced, although not immediately in their second year. Also that they were ridden only by the lightest of light-weight riders of extreme skill. Great care is used to take all weight off the horse's quarters, and its exercise is gradual and limited at that early age.

I added that Pride would not be broken in until she was well into her third year, and in any case she was not the race-horse breed.

Because such interest was shown, I took the precaution of adding: "You do all realize that no one rides my horses uninvited, don't you?" Yes, they realized that.

To the grown man who asked what Pride would do if I sat on her, I repeated that at least she would be severely injured and terrified.

A few hours after I had watched Pride gallop up to the Dovey meadow, a picture of absolute fitness and lithe grace, I had to go out for two or three hours. In that time she was ridden and so died an agonizing but prolonged death.

Unfortunately I knew nothing about it at the time. It was over two days before the terrible truth was known.

When I returned from shopping everything was in order and calm; too calm. The men were busily working. The dogs lay about in the house.

But it is impossible to live closely with animals and not to know when something is amiss. I looked into Nada's eyes. Although her golden tail beat the floor, I asked one of the men: "Is everything all right?"

Yes—he *hoped* so. His manner and reply were odd, but I had to leave it at that. If something of value had been broken I should discover it sooner or later. Broken hearts were not anticipated then; they leave no finger-prints.

It was a day and a half before I knew that something was alarmingly wrong with Pride. She had missed her last two bucket feeds; an unusual occurrence, but an extra feast on milk might explain that.

During the first night of her illness I had heard her whinnying loudly, but thought that she had been left behind in the stable while her mother and Siriol grazed.

The next night I had no such false, but consoling, thoughts. By then I had rushed in the vet. "Pride can't get up." Her temperature of 105° puzzled him. He knew her to be absolutely healthy and fit.

On his third visit, late at night, I stared at the vet: "She's been ridden, hasn't she?"

He admitted that it was the only likely solution. "But what fool would *do* such a thing?"

I asked myself that during Pride's last night, when her screams tore at the heart of Pant Glas. Her agonized death was followed by a post-mortem. It revealed ruptured guts, peritonitis, and pneumonia following severe shock.

By then I had learned from two who had been present exactly what had taken place in my absence. The result was frightened men, lies, evasions and apparently fruitless police inquiries. I was scarcely aware of them.

I saw only the despair in Bess's eyes, and tears trickling down Siriol's nose. A dry sob in a horse's neigh is a dreadful sound.

I did not write again for six months.

To all animal lovers, sooner or later, there comes grief. It is our payment for countless joys received. Death is not tragedy to an animal. It is only we who make it so. There is no long anticipation on their part and their physical pain is alleviated or cut short by us as soon as possible.

There are millions of animals in the world awaiting our care and attention. Few of us take the line: "I could never bear to

have another animal because it will die and I shall be hurt."
Happily, the careful avoidance of pain is left to a few selfish
fanatics; otherwise the world would stop.

Strangely, it was Bess who made the first recovery of
spirit. As soon as I could I mated her again to Llanarth Braint,
now with happily pending results.

Poor Siriol became a changed horse. He would stand, head
hanging in dejection, for hours on end. He began to look old
and his coat lacked its usual sheen. He was vetted but no
specific complaint was diagnosed.

Not until late autumn did his spirits begin to revive. When
I first heard his old, trumpeting neigh it was music to me
indeed. That was when a neighbouring grey mare, Belle, came
to spend the summer with us. But even her arrival did not work
an immediate cure.

One October morning Siriol went to Bess, urging her to
come for a gallop. She flattened her ears and told him to go
away. Undaunted, he sped round on his own, returning to
stare at her.

From that moment his elation has grown. Not once has he
attempted to go near Bess's feeding bucket or hay. When his
own food is finished he walks a few paces away, waiting
patiently for her.

He is only thirteen, so it was more than worrying to see him
age prematurely, losing weight and condition. As Bess has
grown larger so Siriol has put on weight and health. One
night I hope to go into the fields to hear him bellowing the
fact that he is an uncle again.

Because Malpas, the young billy-goat, has been with us
throughout his first year, I had only the vaguest idea when to

expect the kids. But I believe, that Bess has known more accurately. She is essentially maternal and takes an intense interest in births.

The first cry of a kid brings her bustling into the stable, where she leans over the partition to inspect the maternity ward. Her eyes go soft and dewy as she inspects the newcomers. Then out she goes, giving a warm chuckle.

New kittens and puppies are carried to the gate, as soon as their mothers allow it, for Bess's inspection. She doesn't let Siriol get too near while she blows warm benediction over the young. Siriol, who wouldn't hurt a fly, has to wait until I can smuggle them out again for him to see. He leaves Bess safely grazing, then comes to the gate with his tricorn, conspiratorial look.

He really only wants to know what all the fuss was about. "What—*that?*" says his expression. "Can't even see it." He hurries back to Bess, no doubt to explain that he has been hindered by "her".

Talking of devotion and maternal care, Chita is a striking example of those qualities, combined with much common sense. She was terribly undersized when she came to me at five months old. I intended that she should share the fate of my other cats and be neutered. First I must get her strong.

I think she suspected my point of view. For several months she consisted of a pair of sapphire eyes apparently set on the end of a long dark brown tail. There must have been some cat in between, because of the monstrous noise which emanated.

Gradually pale coffee shading defined her body, which remained thin long enough to delude me. Her purr belonged to an aerodrome. Her splendidly shaped brown ears missed no inflexion of my voice. I was happy; she was happy. When sorrow touched me she was on my shoulder, for once silent, pressing her little face against mine.

I had heard that Siamese differed from other cats. I should say that they are a species on their own, with deep intelligence, and retaining the essence of cat. That is true of Chita.

So I delayed her operation past its normal time of five months, having consulted a vet. It would be too difficult to find a properly born mate for her, and I really didn't want kittens. Chita did.

Her house manners were delightful from the first. She ate a little of anything I gave her, sufficient to keep a mouse in full health. It was some time before I discovered that she would share and wolf a good portion of any dog's dinner, except Snip's, and often did so.

When I first brought her home, that microscopic queen of Siam astounded the dogs by saying, in a "Brummy" voice: "El-low!" She still says it; her accent hasn't improved.

Snip, of course, went straight into battle in the manner of any terrier. Chita said: "Downt," and pushed under Snip's stomach, through her hind legs, to reach the more delectable ones of the retrievers, against which she rubbed ecstatically.

Having chastised Snip, I laughed at her blank, outraged expression. There are times when that dog deserves to be laughed at. She has never succeeded in making an enemy of Chita or scaring her in any way.

I was about to make an appointment for Chita with the vet when she developed colic, or some disastrous complaint which threw her into agony; so I thought.

"Ow! Ooo-erow!" On it went, day and night. She rolled on the floor in front of the dogs, repeating the unearthly call. They were most intrigued, especially Snip.

She wanted to go out; she wanted to come in. In—out. "Oooo-er-row-row-row." It was, indeed, a row.

The poor mite seemed to be suffering, and yet—she looked so happy. I telephoned a Siamese breeder, who laughed heartily when I imitated the sound by way of explanation. "Do you think she's swallowed something, Miss Ryan?"

"Not she. It's her mating call."

"But she's only eight months old. She can't *mate* yet."

"She shouldn't. Fourteen months is the right age, but she might. You'll have to watch her."

It was disconcerting advice, especially as I couldn't find Chita anywhere. I went outside to call her many times. At last, from the velvet blackness of the forest, I heard a contralto: "Er-row-row-row-er-row!"

No one was more relieved than I to see Chita coming home two hours later, still singing into the night. But Chita knew very well how to give me the slip when she chose; she chose to on four successive nights, with inevitable results.

Whoever would have thought of the minx having kittens at the age of ten months!

Although I had been told that a pure Siamese queen will mate only with her own kind, I was not convinced. Chita, I was sure, had hobnobbed in the village.

I assisted at the birth of six white kittens. It was a busy night—why always the *night*?

Contrary to common opinion, I never leave a cat or any other animal to have its first family alone. The more gently

99

bred and nurtured the animal, the more reason exists for such primary help.

A lot of rubbish is talked about Nature. Let them live, eat, sleep and play as naturally as possible, but *don't* put a capital "N" to nature when difficulties loom.

I am sure people don't mean to be unkind or neglectful by insisting that, at the time of giving birth, animals are better left entirely to themselves. An experienced mother, possibly, will come through the event unscathed. Even then she would appreciate kindly interest and, if a bitch or cat, laps of warm milk with glucose given, between the arrival of each child.

Chita's sapphire eyes implored me not to leave her, as together we coped with two breach arrivals. Those delayed the final triumph to the total extent of five hours. They would have been miserable and frightening hours for Chita on her own.

"They're beautiful, Chita. But how did you get *white* kittens?" Her reply was a deep, rumbling purr.

I didn't know then that Siamese kittens are born pure white. At a fortnight old the tips of their ears and their tails darken, as if someone had pencilled the edges.

Mystified, again I telephoned Miss Ryan. She told me that Chita must have found a Siamese stud cat, which she most certainly would have done if possible. She didn't know of any local pure Siamese, although she believed that one had been on holiday with his owners some three miles away. I suggested that the cat must have enjoyed his holiday but been rather footsore.

"Oh, that's nothing. They will come for many, many miles when the queen calls."

"Then this one probably walked over from Manchester!"

At five weeks old six perfect seal-point Siamese kittens, with brilliantly blue eyes, enchanted all who saw them. Despite the fact that their father hadn't left his registration papers when he called, there was a long waiting list for them. I was able to choose the best possible homes for them. Ten weeks after their birth I hoped that Chita would gradually become used to her childless state.

Two weeks earlier she had developed her frightful cry. She "Er-rowed" in the forest when not minding the two kittens left to her. But when the last left home she was perfectly content and silent. And well she may have been!

I, too, was speechless when I recognized her condition. The wail I had so nicely attributed to her maternal grief had been nothing of the sort. Chita was pregnant again.

This time she blew some Siamese theories sky high by having six tabby kittens, some with white markings. They were just as dearly loved and, by eight weeks old, all had good homes, with the exception of the silver-grey tabby, Lissa, who had crept into my heart.

By now Chita was a picture of romping health. Her own frail kittenhood was forgotten. I realized that any creature, so intended to be a mother, could not kindly be neutered. But I firmly resolved to cut out this Nature business.

Intently I listened for her first lascivious wail. It came, right enough, but as we were snow-bound. No drifts would have stopped her cunning ways, so doors and windows were shut and kept shut. By the time the snow had gone, Chita had cooled down, for the next three weeks.

Then I took her to Miss Ryan's famous stud cat. She came

home speechless, which endeared me to her more than ever.

In her absence Lissa had occupied herself in many ingenious ways. She had washed the three retrievers from head to tail and had learned to roll an egg over the edge of the table, putting the contents to good and palatable use. She was delighted to have her mother back and spent an entire evening washing her.

I have noticed that whenever a dog barks, Chita chimes. Even if she is asleep, a mellow sound, rather like a grand-father-clock with a faint whirr before the half-hour is noted, issues from her, increasing in volume.

The worst of having four dogs, instead of one, is that you either have to go about in a pack or single one out for special attention. The pack movement is excellent here because there are many safe walks well away from flocks of sheep.

Any one of my dogs is good about sheep; that is, they ignore them. But I should never trust four of the most saintly dogs to ramble loose among sheep, especially in the lambing season. That, unfortunately, coincides with hare activities.

One day I was horrified to see that a hare had led my pack straight through a neighbour's sheep. The line was too swift to harm the sheep, even by mild alarm. But I knew that once the hunt was over the dogs would return to me, in ones or twos, and then the sheep might run.

I waited anxiously until the scent gave out. Only a foolish optimist would call a dog in the middle of a hunt, expecting immediate obedience. Then I whistled, adding a call in my sternest voice.

Three of them came at once, scurrying through the offending gap which was mended later that day.

"Get on—get on, now. You know you're trespassing."

As Snip passed through, heeding my loveless tone, she rolled up her eyes until they were nearly pure white; a habit she has when anticipating the worst. When she wears that "Oh Lord, preserve us!" look, I adore her but don't mention the fact.

Snip, Bracken and Sheena all present. Where was Nada? Mother of Bracken and Sheena's grandmother, Nada always took her responsibilities heavily. It was she who helped me to impress upon the others about this dreadful sheep business when we first came to Wales. I wondered if the old darling had gone three miles round by road, rather than let me see her coming through sheep.

I waited for some time on my side of the fence, the others at my heels. Then I saw her. Never did a golden retriever look more embarrassed. As she drew nearer, her expressive dark eyes were raised to mine in dire apology, before her glance returned to the region of her hind legs. Then her expression grew rapt.

Butting her tummy in fruitless quest was a very young lamb in black stockings. It insisted on calling Nada "Ma-aa". And Nada loved it.

It was five years since a young creature had needed her in that capacity. She nosed it gently away with adoration in her eyes, until she remembered me.

Nada knew too well the penalties attached to chasing sheep, or looking at them. She had relayed that information to the younger dogs, especially to Snip, many times. But what happened when a sheep chased her? She looked at me in mute appeal.

Snip had begun to bounce. Bracken and Sheena were ready to welcome a new child to Pant Glas, especially one brought there by Nada. I thought quickly.

"Nada, stay where you are. I'm taking the dogs home. On guard!"

The others followed me reluctantly. Nada was delighted with her charge. I quite expected her to have come into milk by the time I returned to her; she is like that. But I was rather worried so ran half a mile home.

Supposing a shepherd saw Nada and thought that she was worrying the lamb. I didn't console myself with the obvious thought that shepherds are never short-sighted or daft. But I knew that the lamb would be perfectly safe.

Safe indeed it was. By the time I reached them Nada had been accosted, from a distance, by the lamb's outraged parent. Nada was in an awful quandary. Every time she made an attempt to return the child to its mother, the sheep bleated and ran off in a wide circle.

"Nada, come here."

The lamb came with her.

"Good girl. Bring it to me."

That order she understood and was delighted to obey.

I let Nada come under the fence with the lamb, then told her to wait. But I couldn't catch the lamb by myself, so had to rescind the order. Eventually Nada nosed the mite to me. I picked it up, scrambled over the wire fence and walked towards the mother, who ran off, bleating: "Mair-mairder," in a most ridiculous fashion.

I put the lamb down and went back to Nada, who watched anxiously, her head twisting slowly one way and then the other.

We waited for a few minutes before the sheep, sensing that violent danger had passed, reclaimed her own.

The lamb showed less enthusiasm, I thought, for its own mother than for Nada's golden awning.

Nada gave me a swift, anxious look. Then she knew that everything was all right—very all right—and that I loved her dearly.

One could mistakenly suspect Snip of being devoid of maternal feelings. She's a pugnacious little person at times and she dislikes all small children. Heaven protect the cat who jumps near her when she's asleep! Hens leave her entirely nonplussed; she doesn't know which end of them to suspect. On several occasions a whirr of feathers in her face has had curious effect; Snip had ducked her head, turned tail and gone home. I always hope the hens won't try her too far.

But with anything new-born Snip is a shivering mass of sentimental nonsense. She screws her head round so far that she has only one eye with which to view the newcomers. Her eyes grow positively moist as she listens keenly to the suck, suck, suck.

I was agitated when Snip inadvertently saw Chita's day-old kittens in the writing-room. Rather than make bad blood by shooing her out at once, I let her sit on my bed. She was a model of rectitude, so was allowed to call each morning at the same time, duly chaperoned by me.

On the fourth day I ventured to hold one of the precious white kittens for Snip's inspection. She lifted its tail carefully, dealing with it as she would with one of her own puppies.

She had a litter of four hunt terrier puppies in her first year at Pant Glas. She was an ideal mother and presented one of her sons at eight weeks old to the Plas Machynlleth Kennels, where he still lives and works in perpetual happiness.

Snip loved that white kitten. What is more, she intended to feed it, and did for a short time. I was astounded to find that she had come into milk, although she had not whelped for over three years.

Rather than risk upsetting one kitten's digestion, I rang the changes. Each kitten in turn had brief but competent treatment by Snip, until they were three weeks old. Chita didn't mind. She just washed off Snip's influence and repeated the work.

It seems logical that such a community should have its own welfare centre. Certainly Pant Glas has one, which is completely free of human organization. But a mere human, observing these matters, could learn much.

In pre-natal concerns they keep to their own kind in the main. The handsome cat, China, who has no sex but much sense, spends the last weeks of Chita's repeated pregnancies in guarding her.

If cloud and rain disperse while Chita is asleep, China takes trouble to find and wake her, propelling her into the warmest patch of sunshine. They sit in it for a time, when China wanders off to look for something. Having found it, he then lures or pushes Chita towards a clump of grass, evidently containing magical properties. He stands by while Chita nibbles daintily. Then together they sharpen claws on a tree before gliding off to their single or mutual pursuits.

China adores wooden posts or fences, on which he sits for hours, white sentinel of Pant Glas. From such a vantage point he is able to see everything of importance to him.

Suddenly he will jump, rush downhill, cross the brook and dart to a hedgerow which is in view of the post he has left.

How he could have seen an unsuspecting field mouse from such a distance I never know. Within seconds he brings it back, dead. He is a swift killer. Then, if Chita's time is drawing near, he singles her out, laying the trophy at her feet. She swears out thanks to him and he returns to his watch-tower.

When Chita's kittens are old enough to appreciate such gifts, China makes many unselfish sacrifices on their part, not without a struggle. I have seen him look longingly at a dead mouse or vole, carry it off for a distance until his better nature conquers. Quickly he takes it to Chita and the kittens.

When the kittens are four or five weeks old, and ripe for active fun, China brings his gifts to them alive. This evidently costs him more, for he rarely stays to watch the fate of his victim. He hurries off, as if he couldn't bear to see incompetence at the helm.

Chita is well able to teach her own children the rudiments of sport. But she is not averse to such outside help, especially when she's busy.

At six weeks old the kittens are taken by both cats to hunt in likely spots. For practice on quick springing to kill they often start on Michael's tail, found lashing the hay. The kittens, swift to observe sound and action, leap towards this tempting movement. Although old Michael utters violent "merrows", he never hurts anyone. He goes on lashing his tail until he can bear it no longer. Then, invoking the Devil, he moves out of paw-shot.

Then the kittens, having grasped the idea, look round for

further movement, their direction guided tactfully by their mother and China.

The competency of the midwife, Siriol, is already known. What that cob doesn't know about foals and foaling will be learnt in a few weeks' time. Already he and Bess lie down for the better part of sunny mornings. A horse in Siriol's condition of expectancy can't be too careful—of his mare.

I have been wondering a good deal about Jane, the only sheep here. From whom will she learn the necessary facts of birth and maternal care? The neighbours' sheep are too far away to pass on such information. She has grown aloof and no longer presses her head into my knees. Her habit of sleeping with the goats at night has been broken. She mingles with them until they go indoors. Then, a white shadow, she moves away with the horses to be engulfed by darkness.

Last night I knew that such fears could be discounted. It was dark when I went out to see that all was well. The goats slept or chewed the cud among warm straw. The horses had gone to a sheltered spot they favoured. Michael's tabby form moved silently from the barn towards a wooden plank which connects the knoll bank with my bedroom—wise cat!

Then I became aware that Niall had risen to her knees. While I checked that water buckets were full and clean, Niall went outside, as if she had some wearisome duty to attend. I followed her out.

There they were: Jane and Niall. The sheep and the goat, heads pressed together, were turning in a slow circle. I watched, intrigued.

This was no mere game. Niall thought too much of her own comfort to frolic where the wind was cold and on a moonless night. At thirteen years of age she knows that home is best. But at two years old, and softly nurtured, Jane had a deal to learn. Who better than the aged leader of the herd to teach her?

Niall, who shows no affection for Jane nor notices her when the herd is active, had gone out deliberately to tell the lone sheep something which she should know.

When they had circled from left to right three times, they turned in an opposite direction for three revolutions, still head to head. Niall then gently nibbled Jane's ears—or did she whisper?

I felt they needed only a cauldron from which arose a foul smell, snakes and toads in quantity, to complete the witches' scene.

Presently Jane, facing the upper fields, was butted off in that direction by Niall; full, surely, of supremely useful knowledge. Niall, with beard lowered gravely to the ground, rejoined her family.

Just before I went indoors I was surprised to see Michael scurry back, past the outbuildings in the direction which Jane had taken.

Now, that cat always likes his nights in the house. Could it be that he, an emissary, had watched Jane's lonely plight and, recognizing it, told Niall that she was needed? For certainly Jane had made no sound.

It was well past midnight when Michael came through my bedroom window and, having turned round three times on my bed, settled to a long and well-earned sleep.

I could have imagined the causes; most certainly I did not imagine the facts.

Chapter Eight

THERE is something *muffled* about a cat. Its clean thoughts lie hidden behind impersonal slits. Just as you are about to slink off, feeling your rank inferiority, a purr like an engine tells you to stay where you are—for a moment or so.

You might be detained by the apathetic touch of an outstretched paw, or merely intrigued because, without apparent reason, you have been drawn into focus.

It is ineffectual to say that you like cats, hate them, fear, adore or are allergic to them. The cat defines your status, and quickly.

"Puss, puss! Oh, the darling! Come here, my sweet. You know I love you."

How would you react to such a sloppy introduction? You'd excuse yourself on the slightest pretext, wouldn't you? Then why be offended when, with one bound, the loved one—*loved* in that short time!—darts to inaccessible cover?

Nine times out of ten you will be quietly watched. Long before you realize that there is a cat within sight, your entire character and latent tendencies will be known. It's a disconcerting thought; more so the fact that cats don't always keep this knowledge to themselves.

No one arrives at Pant Glas without clear assessment. There are usually at least five pairs of eyes to retain, or pass on, the knowledge.

I don't believe that cats estimate as we do. Good, bad or indifferent to them have little to do with moral code.

They watch with scorn the dogs who fling themselves in mad ecstasy, indiscriminately, at visitors, or who are offended by a rough tone.

It would be a waste of time for one cat to tell another, since all cats *know*. But I think that, where advisable, they pass on messages to the others, at discretion.

Their messages must run on these lines: "There's someone arriving who will stay too long. They will want doors and windows closed." Or possibly: "This one is against the life here—our life. They won't influence *her*, but don't crowd round."

This could explain a curious reaction on the part of goats on occasions. I have two relatives who call infrequently. Their first visit to Pant Glas coincided with the total disappearance of Niall, Bambi and Belinda. At that time they were my entire herd.

Months later the same people came again, with cameras. All I know is that, when those films were developed, the results must have been an astonishing variety of rear views woven into the darkest shadows of dark bushes.

There was one exception: Panda. She, the black and white half-Persian, whose black pupils can blaze to a complete circle or vanish into a slit befitting the finest needle, is notoriously shy. One crunch of a foreign foot on the path and she has fled—for the day.

On that particular day she was much in evidence. She appeared on every gatepost in turn, she lay stretched out in the sun, she used her magnificent tail in the manner of an intriguing *danseuse*.

When the visitors exclaimed: "Isn't she *gorgeous*!" she murmured softly: "And-*yew*, merrand-*yew*," extending the benefit of her pure white undercarriage for their delectation.

I knew then that the minx had been up to something. Watching her pose for her photographs, in costly numbers, I wondered how many animals would share that distinction. Not one, it proved, except for those obscene rear shadows.

My suspicions grew when I saw Michael leaving the hay for a sunnier spot. Panda rushed to him and back he went—back into the shadows.

She returned to the visitors, Supreme Empress. "So sorry the others aren't at home," said her bewitching, false manner. She couldn't so dispose of the dogs. So she treated them to unusual toleration, weaving through their legs with complete abandon. The dogs, dumbfounded, treated her with a respect she didn't deserve.

There was absolutely no excuse for such cat-engendered behaviour on the part of so many absent animals. Those relatives are perfectly nice, country loving people who wouldn't dream of hurting an animal or its feelings.

Six months later they came again. What happened? The drain—in those days the one and only drain—became blocked. They spent hours in digging and delving for us and, finally, restoring us to some means of sanitary living.

Having dug up the front terrace and a large portion of garden, the chief trouble was discovered to be near the house. Only a few inches from there a whole heap of horrid mush had conglomerated round a clothes peg and—half a rabbit's foot. It was the last object which made me look round for Panda. That repulsive plaything had been distinctly hers as recently as that very morning.

What vile inspiration had caused the drain to become blocked, to such arduous and back-breaking purpose?

Looking up, I saw Panda on top of the water tank, serenely washing her face. The goats, horse and lamb were mingling near the stables, as they do at milking times. But our visitors couldn't stay to photograph them.

As soon as they had gone, having been thanked for their labours, Panda jumped down from the tank, going to her feeding place, an obscure corner of the loft over the kitchen. I showed her the offending portion of rabbit's foot: "I believe this is yours?"

Hers—*that* object? Disdainfully she stepped down to the kitchen, settling on the edge of the table while I prepared food for them all. Her expression told me: "I shall eat with them tonight—slightly apart, naturally."

"Panda, have you worked a mischief today?"

The perpendicular slits in her green eyes widened until there was much black and little green. She really is a pretty creature. I wonder if *Jezebel* would have been a better name for her?

For they do work a mischief now and then. It puts the human race into perspective. Why shouldn't animals laugh at us sometimes? We laugh at them often enough.

Their sense of humour varies in quality and depth as much as ours. I have already described Siriol as a horse with a personality. His humour is highly developed, but dry.

I can trust him with a small child or with anyone's grandmother on their first ride. He moves as if he carried eggs loose in the saddle and is aware of the fact.

But let someone mount him, having a false idea that they ride well; he is the first to disillusion. He needs no loose flapping of reins about his neck, or hands grasping too tightly, to tell him the calibre of his passenger.

He tolerates a walk, followed by a gentle trot. That second pace also reveals much to me, often too late. Having been told again by the rider that any horse is manageable, this one especially so, I don't like to suggest that they would be better to dismount. "Take him steadily up the field as far as the gate," I say weakly.

The gate is never reached. A few paces short of it he and the passenger part company. There is nothing vicious or unduly alarming about his buck. It's as if he said quietly: "Off you get, my dear. You ride me again when you've had a few lessons."

Only with the very self-assured does he let them flop from saddle to the ground. Usually he offers a strong neck by which he lowers his victim with the utmost care.

Then he returns to me, looking rather pained. It is as if he were trying to explain that his rider "took a voluntary". I look at the anxious creases over his tricorn eyes: "There was nothing voluntary about that, my boy."

Having inquired anxiously and made profound apologies, I take the rascal for a short way myself. He knows what is wanted without any aids being applied. After a hearty leap over the ditch, he puts in four or five spurts, which include a buck or so—the armchair type and easy to sit—returning to the visitor, breathing like an outraged dragon.

I explain that he is in one of his moods and, by mutual agreement, he is unsaddled and turned free. He keeps up the farce for a few minutes, galloping and flinging out his hind legs in a most fearsome fashion.

But creep out to see him moments later and he will be nibbling or lying beside Bess, perhaps having his chin tickled by a goat's tail—a never-ending source of satisfaction to him.

Those who are nicely nervous, professing to ride only a little, I can entrust to Siriol with all equanimity. He proves himself to be a patent safety, confidential cob.

In private life he is a jester. It is quite unsafe to take out a deck-chair if he hovers near, showing plenty of white to his eye. You will place the chair just so, prepared for a nice, easy laze. I'm sorry to say that, in all probability, you will sit on the ground—suddenly. For that dear bay cob will have moved the chair in a split second while you were in the act of sitting down.

Alternatively, you could sit down in safety. Just when you're feeling drunk with the utter peace of it all, you might be alarmed to feel a plastic bowl bang down on your head.

It would be one of the goats' feeding bowls. Usually these are collected after a meal. But occasionally one is overlooked—or stolen. Siriol has a passion for them, full or empty. Possibly their varied colours attract him, or the plastic material is easy for him to grab and to carry for some distance. A nice fool he looks, too, with a red, yellow or blue washing-up bowl, its use now twice transferred, held over his face like a gas mask.

I believe he first developed this trick to entertain the filly. Nothing delighted her more than to see her uncle trot towards her with such an amazing toy. Now it has become a permanent obsession with him.

His beloved black Bess is unamused by such capers. She is sweet-tempered on all occasions, reliable under all conditions, but—she has no sense of humour. Although Siriol is devoted to her, he has given up trying to make her laugh.

If he must crack a joke it is done with the horned, Anglo-Nubian goat, Belinda. Of all the goats her sense of humour equals Siriol's.

On a dancing day in early spring—when the wind is piping mad and keen—Belinda twirls round on her hind legs, before diving at Siriol with her head. No harm is done. Siriol then nibbles her horns, or runs his teeth lightly up and down her spine.

This would go on indefinitely, if Belinda had no train to catch. While she has been fooling with Siriol the other goats have gone without her. Suddenly she realizes this and, with a bleat of horror, makes up for lost time.

The Goat Train has no predictable time-table—unless you are a goat. To the best of my knowledge it is governed by weather and seasons. It is part of the solemn function of a goat's daily life here. It must not—simply must not—be missed. This is what happens:

The station of departure is usually the stables. Occasionally it will start from a sheltered spot in the fields which is being used as a rest centre. Goats don't rest for long in the day-time. When they do they are very thorough about it, as in most of their activities. Their sound sleep has to be heard to be believed.

Niall, the white leader, rises by her knees to full height. She points her beard to the sky, then lowers it to within an inch of the ground. She moves slowly down the bank, saying: "Urh-urh." I gather it means "Come on", because of its immediate effect.

One by one the herd drifts after her, each giving the impression of not actually doing so. One turns left, another right, but only while Niall nibbles at a hawthorn bush or larch fence. As soon as she reaches the lower path she is followed by the herd which, at present, is twelve strong. Nose to tail, their pace is then governed by hers.

She ambles in a direct line down the valley, gathering speed as the lower fields come into view. She and her train don't stop to eat again until the farthest point is reached. They spend several hours working their way slowly homeward, always under the leader's direction. But should a sudden and heavy shower break, Niall gathers steam and the train becomes the Goat Express.

I grow conscious of the Goat Train only when someone has missed it.

"What *is* the matter with that goat?" a guest might ask.

"She's missed the train."

"*What?*"

"The Goat Train." There isn't time to explain all, for we should be left with plaintive bleats for hours. "Did you happen to see which way it went?"

A blank stare is perhaps all I deserve. I am more explicit: "Did you notice if the goats went up or downhill?"

The belief had been that goats went in all directions. I correct that idea by taking the bereaved goat and the visitor on a train hunt.

117

"Sylvan, how could you be so stupid! *You* know what time the train leaves; I don't."

"Mair-e-air—m-air."

"I know, dear. But if you'd only pay more attention you wouldn't waste so much of my time."

This brings forth the same response, but usually there is pity in the glance of my human friend; pity or anxiety. At this point I am sometimes asked: "You don't think that you live *too* much alone, do you?"

"Alone!" Stepping over two smaller friends, who have rushed to meet me, I murmur from habit: "Hello, Caroline —Mrs. Henrietta! No, I wouldn't say that I live alone at all."

"No?" comes the uneasy reply, followed by silence, possibly because of the gradient, or interruptive bleats.

From the top of the knoll there is a good view of the higher land. There isn't a goat in sight in the Cader Idris, Cardigan or Dovey fields. The oak woods show only the two cobs. I suggest that we take Sylvan down the valley. Already she is tugging in that direction.

There are more heart-rending cries as we emerge into void fields below. Sylvan has lost confidence in my sense of direction. Once lost, they cling to that idea for longer than is sensible. Suddenly I see a trail of white blended into foliage.

I lug her along then thrust her forward. At last she sees and runs towards the herd. Gazelle, her mother, comes to meet her, making an apt sound: "Larn yer!"

At milking time, or when weather and inclinations urge, the train comes back again. Slowly, shunting up the valley, with various stops dictated by Niall, they move in single file.

Woe betide anyone who thinks to take the lead. Niall's head is harder than any pair of horns when she chooses to use it.

In their second year with me I took Bambi and Belinda, at discreet intervals, to the billy-goat who lived a mile away. These were occasions for much giggling among the bridesmaids left at the lower gate until our return. Only in the cause of true romance would they have waited in one spot to greet the blushing one. That, by the way, was not the goat. I was boiled to beetroot colour by hanging on to the collar of a traffic-shy monster.

As a car approached I was propelled through the air, usually landing in a well-thorned hedge or in a ditch with the goat on top of me.

Last summer Dovey Malpas reigned supreme here, monarch of all he surveyed. That doesn't mean to say that Niall relinquished her leadership; although as winter developed she sometimes designated Bambi to take her place on any walk she was too fulsome to enjoy.

And a nice mess Bambi made of it, more often than not. Her condition was no easier than Niall's but, because she is six years old and Niall thirteen, there was good reason for Bambi at least to try.

Her crocodile became a disjointed circle. Someone ran back to see what Niall was doing, getting nipped in the ear for her curiosity. Having dispatched the erring one, Niall settled down, chewing the cud and ruminating on the inefficiency — the *irre-goatancy*—of youth.

The one member of the family here to have the best of all worlds is Jane, the sheep. Moving with the goats as one of them, eating and sleeping with them, she retains at all times what she obviously considers to be her slightly higher status. Since she isn't likely to know of it, her opinion can't stem from Biblical prejudice.

When Niall indicates that the herd shall turn left, Jane has already anticipated the move or ignored it, until she seems likely to be left behind. Then, with an odd hunch of the shoulders, peculiar to her, she hurries on to wherever her friends are.

Her deep passion is horses. She will shelter from sun or rain under Bess or Siriol and graze with them by the hour. Strangely, this rarely entails missing the Goat Train, although she is often the last to catch it. But if the lure of the horse has proved too great and the train has gone on its daily route to somewhere special and nowhere in particular, Jane will make the best of it, returning to the horses. But she's always on that train when it comes home.

I have watched her artful ways, time and again. To face the homeward bound train evidently means disgrace. Neither must she turn in front of it, usurping the lead. Niall would have something unpleasant to say about that.

If the train has gone north, over the knoll and to the highest grazing, then joining it from the rear is a simple matter of strategy. She bustles along the outer boundary until she can emerge nonchalantly, in time to form the last coach.

But if the train returns from the south there is the acute embarrassment of a bottle-neck. The land is the shape of an hour-glass. On the tree-laced path no vehicles can pass; neither can a defaulting sheep appear to be coming when, in fact, she is going.

Jane runs for a short distance, stops and listens. She looks at a high bank on her right; to her left is the fern-guarded brook. I have seen the keen calculation in her almond-shaped eyes as she glances from one side to the other.

Possibly the sound of hoofs on pebbles has told her what she wants to know. The train might stop for water before the final rise which will bring her into view. Or it might leap up the bank, for a tasty morsel or so on the way. It could come straight up the path, slowly but non-stop.

It is not easy for over a cubic yard of white wool to eliminate itself. By standing stock still at the crucial moment, Jane manages to do just that.

If the others are on the bank or path, Jane becomes a white shadow against white stone, in the brook. If heads are lowered to water, she darts up the bank, to mingle later with the rest. Never does she meet them face to face on the centre of the path.

Once I saw Niall change her course suddenly. One moment she was nibbling at the bank, the next she realized a sudden thirst. It was unfortunate that Jane, who was slyly admiring her own reflection, should be two paces uphill.

Niall lowered her head and charged. Jane, taken by surprise, was shot to the far side of the water in one shocked movement. Naturally she landed on her feet, bleating. It seemed rather hard, after she had taken so much deceptive care.

Jane arrived home by train with the others, but Niall remained testy with her for the rest of that evening. Perhaps she said: "Make up your mind. You can be half-horse or half-goat, but you can't be both."

When it is considered that Jane began life in the house, sleeping on my bed until she was old enough to lie with the dogs, her singular attitude is understandable. She knows where most kitchen utensils are kept, and that if larch is put on the fire, five paces back are indicated. When the dogs have a friendly mêlée in the fields, she doesn't retreat; she joins in.

She never appears to consort with Gazelle, who had a similar domestic beginning. Gazelle, who once considered herself to be a golden retriever, has become a goat. Jane, who from the first knew that she was a sheep, retains that knowledge with a glazed superiority. And well she may, for with it goes a marked intelligence.

The stable doors are rarely closed at night. But if blustery weather makes it advisable and Jane is a late grazer, she is furious to come home, finding herself shut out. She bleats, and if immediate human response is not given, she kicks the stable door in no uncertain manner.

When life is going her way—it usually does—she chews the cud and, unless a mouth deliberately raised at the corners indicates any other emotion, she *smiles*.

A cat always makes Jane smile. She adores them. The affection is mutual. She pushes them round with her nose, wriggling her tail with joy. Michael was very suspicious of this treatment at first. Now he goes back for more and often singles Jane out, leaning his tabby pattern affectionately against her.

I adhere to my original opinion—that a flock of sheep is the silliest gathering in the animal world. I am sorry I feel bound to define that last word! But single out any one of them to live with or near you and an intelligence is shown, far in excess of a well-trained sheep-dog.

It is in a dog's nature to please and to work according to its breed and training. Not so with a sheep. Jane hasn't been taught parlour tricks, but she has acquired plenty. She sways to music of her choice. She used to weave through two complete sets of horses' legs, from fore to hind; a novel way of scratching her ribs. Now I doubt if the horse exists who could so accommodate her. She takes a wicked delight in sitting down suddenly on a hen. Strangely, the hen is never hurt and often returns the compliment, after extracting itself, by perching on her back. I have never seen the cocks so demean themselves.

Jane is first to give visible warning of approaching visitors. Her ears are thrust forward in the direction of a sound which is seconds later in reaching the dogs.

Often it is Jane who tells the goats to take courage. One day an outsize Pyrenean mountain dog called with his owners. He was allowed free range. The goats, who are never cowardly, were nonplussed. They formed a complete circle round Jane, possibly because she makes a pneumatic centre.

As the dog, intent on ravishingly new scents, drew nearer, the circle moved backwards, horned goats to the fore. Suddenly the dog looked up to see the strange group hovering some feet away. His first idea of going to inspect was tempered by wisdom. He went on sniffing the grass.

This was too much for Jane. To be attacked, *en masse*, by such a monster would not be without compensation. Humans would rush out, squawking and waving their arms. The hens would cry "Wherk!" and go berserk, and there would be a general uproar. She would have something interesting to watch while, from a safe vantage point, she chewed the cud. But to be *ignored* by the enemy was the final outrage.

With a woolly shove, Jane broke from the circle and menaced towards the stranger. Unlike goats, she raises her head high when there is real business to be negotiated. Unfortunately the dog wasn't paying attention, so Jane stamped her feet within inches of his tail. He went on sniffing.

A sheep's face has little scope for expression. But in that final moment of exasperation I saw, or thought I saw, her mouth tighten. She hunched her shoulders deliberately before walking round him and stamping her feet in front of his engrossed nose.

Poor Jane had to repeat the effort twice before he looked up, staring blankly at her. I shouldn't like to belittle Jane's show of bravery by suggesting that, by then, she knew that she was dealing with a fool. She closed the last inches, bleated into his nostrils sharply: "Mer!" and stamped again.

At last that dog, the size of a small donkey, grasped the idea that he wasn't wanted, and scurried off.

Jane trotted back to the herd. The goats were stiff with admiration. Niall's benediction took the form of grazing hip to hip with Jane in a safer vicinity.

That incident was typical of the way in which Jane uses some of her intelligence to ingratiate herself upon the people who matter. Whether it be a herd of goats, a string of horses, a pride of cats, a pack of dogs or a puzzlement of humans, they all come under her spell sooner or later.

No one can accuse Jane of fawning, although she has her own peculiar standards of loyalty. I can call her until I'm breathless and she remains studiously deaf, if it suits her. But if I want to milk goats and they are missing it's a different matter. I call Niall and several others by name; there is neither sound nor sight of them. Repeating the call I hear Jane answering: "Mer." At once I know where to find the herd.

The goats seem to take such betrayal as a matter of course. Knowing that the game is up, they saunter towards me, allowing the traitress, Jane, to mingle with them, unshoved and unbutted. Perhaps they have resigned themselves to having a flock within a herd.

For a flock she seems to be. She is almost too versatile and able, to be just one sheep. Having derived immense benefits from watching closely the peculiarities of cats, dogs, hens, humans, horses and goats, she will have much profound knowledge to pass on to her children.

That day is not far off. Already Jane spends many hours dreaming beside Bess. The mare and sheep have far-away expressions in their eyes as they nibble and knit the grass. Siriol and the billy goat are really not wanted at the moment. The visiting ram left months ago, wise chap!

Siriol pushes a little extra hay towards Bess, who flattens her ears in an unusual manner. That's all the thanks he gets for solicitude.

Although late winter snow is on the mountains, and the green valley waits tensely for its cue, the animals know which phase of the moon and precisely which incoming tide will bring the individual miracles of new life.

North and east winds can whip these foreign grasses to a paleness which will not endure. The white wind, rushing through the forests, can only madden itself with grief, which has no foothold here.

"Wherk-uk-uk-uk!"

"Yew-tew? Merroo!" Chita is enchanted by the news. "Ah-doodle-ah-doodle-ah-doodle-oodle-ooo!"

Niall gives a low, wicked chuckle. She knows that Pewter's boast couldn't extend to the goats; to the others, possibly.

Chapter Nine

ALL the animals at Pant Glas are good mixers; all except Snip. Her terrier teeth are bared at visitors unless they happen to be human ones. Then charm oozes out of her.

Panda has the reverse tendency. She will purr round the four legs of any strange animal, so long as it isn't Chita. But let them possess only two legs and a voice which cries: "Oh, what a beautiful cat!" and, usually, with ears flattened she has fled to safer haunts. I sometimes wonder how that cat came to be bred by me.

Last summer Belle Jones came to stay for several months, because she was short of grazing at home. She is a grey cob mare, of considerable weight and is not young.

She has dinner-plate feet which fling in all directions when she wants to get somewhere in a hurry. She has the most terrific neigh, mostly soprano. She could well be a *prima donna* with a "code in her dose".

Her most ecstatic call sounds like: "One fine day I'll see you . . ." Madam Butterfly is discounted as she drops to a nasal snort before thundering to meet whomever she had in mind.

When Belle arrived she had Siriol in mind. His rich bay coat, gleaming in the evening sunshine, brought out all the music in her. With a clatter of hoofs, she rushed to him, leaping the brook in an unorthodox but effective manner. Siriol had replied to her song with a genial trumpeting.

I was uneasy. Supposing Bess became jealous or Belle attacked her. My fears soon dispersed as I hurried towards their meeting-place, then stood to watch.

All three horses were previously acquainted. My two often stopped to pass the time of day when being ridden past Belle's home field. Until then their association had been a head and neck one.

Bess stood aside while Siriol pranced forward to meet his new love. He seemed to kiss Belle on both cheeks before breathing heavily into her white mane. Then he moved adroitly while Belle flung her hind legs in about a dozen directions at once. Siriol had spent much time with mares before he came to me, for which fact I was then thankful.

When Belle had four feet on the ground but was still quivering with excitement, Bess went solemnly forward and smelt her nose. Bess didn't stay long just then because Siriol was displaying polygamous tendencies by circling dizzily round his pair of beauties. Bess nibbled the grass while she waited.

After more ribald behaviour, it was Belle who drew Siriol's attention to the fact that there were three of them. They went up to Bess, who proved to be the perfect hostess. Leaving Belle on Siriol's off side, she walked calmly behind the pair of them, taking up her place beside Siriol.

Then Bess inclined her head across him towards Belle. It was an entirely gracious gesture. In an instant the three cobs lifted their heads and were off in perfect line.

Siriol blew a fanfare of trumpets, Belle held to her theme song: "One fine day I'll see you . . . Brrrh-snuck!" They

Michael, stolidly minding his own business

China, white sentinel of Pant Glas

Chicken feed for China

Family gathering

Connoisseurs of Grieg

A joke between friends

Pant Glas, the blue-green valley

Goat train terminus

Sylvan has great expectations

A cat always makes Jane smile

Standing room only?

Belle Jones pays a visit

A seat out of the sun

Family at work . . .

. . . and at play

Lissa's turn to make the tea

Then time for meditation

Beyond the oak woods, the Dovey Estuary and the sea

Time off on Borth sands

Jane, with her whitest of white lambs

Llanarth Siriol, confidential cob

Au revoir

galloped fast over a wide acreage. In fact, they took the very route which Bess had first travelled with Siriol when he showed her over her new home.

Bess maintained a dignified silence, but was not a degree slower than the others. Black, burnished copper, white; they looked magnificent, thrusting their colours before the rays of a splendid sunset.

I can sympathize with the uninitiated about horses' colouring. I have no idea why a perfectly white horse should always be "grey", or why a chestnut should be termed a "bay" because of black mane and tail.

Yet white "white" ponies are permissible, which is such a good thing, otherwise Cinderella's pantomimes would be ruined annually.

I fear we must claim these affectations as our own. They might have sounder reasons than the awfulness of calling a sofa a "couch", or a table napkin a "serviette".

I do remember bridling like an affronted hen when someone referred to my dear old Ballygiblin as "your dark brown horse". I was too speechless at the time to point out in a chilled tone that he happened to have a black mane and black tail. When I had recovered from the shock I was able to laugh at myself. He would have been the best horse I've known had he been pale pink.

Although the animals are good mixers, there are times when it is discreet to segregate a visitor. This was so when Pippin came for four days. His manners were impeccable, especially as he had never left his mistress's pocket or shoulder for any length of time.

Pippin slept with me in the writing-room, because had he

joined his mistress in the house we feared there were too many curiosity mongers to get scent of him.

I was warned that he would probably bite me. He did; the tip of my nose when I got into bed. After that we were the best of friends.

I spent several worried hours, wondering if I had overlain Pippin, when he appeared in some remarkable place. My nose was still tingling from his scissile attack when I realized that he had darted down the sheets to play with my toes.

The knowledge was not reassuring. For half an hour I suffered only by anticipation—the curse of our species— when, thinking that Pippin must have fallen asleep on my feet, I was astonished to see him peering boldly into my eyes.

"Hello, darling. Do you like it here?"

My voice either amused or confounded him, because he did loops and boops all over the bed, returning to see what had made such a din.

Gradually his little eyes lost their brightness as need of sleep overcame him. My need was greater, but I still had not ventured to put out the light. He let me run a forefinger over his silken *café au lait* body without demur, as he curled into the eiderdown.

I read half a chapter of a novel when nature urged me to follow Pippin's example. Before putting out the light I glanced down at the sleeper. He wasn't there.

Quite noiselessly Pippin had arrived on the top book-shelf and was sitting on *The Oxford Dictionary of Quotations*, washing his face.

"Sweet, do come down and go to sleep, there's a good boy."

With exquisite grace he leapt into the air, somersaulting on to Rudyard Kipling's *Thy Servant a Dog*, from whence he sat regarding me curiously.

Assured that at least his literary tastes showed discernment, I decided to leave Pippin where he was but in darkness.

The next morning I was roused by his mistress who had brought me a cup of tea.

"Heavens! Where's Pippin?" My hands groped wildly round the bed.

She laughed heartily. "When you've drunk that I'll tell you."

"But I might have squashed him in the night. Do look for him."

She assured me that there was no need. I was wearing Pippin in my hair. He was still sound asleep. Not a nest of robins in my hair—a nest of *weasel*.

Pippin the weasel had a wonderful three months with his devoted mistress, from the age of one day when he was found in a lane, abandoned by his mother. She took him to Surrey to stay with friends and there her tragedy—not Pippin's—happened.

One moment the weasel, who already had an appointment to appear on television, was with her, enchanting everyone who met him. The next he was nowhere to be found.

A distracted mistress spent the rest of the day searching and calling his name. She didn't sleep at all that night. Instead she lay thinking of a trapped or tortured weasel who whimpered for safety and his adored one.

Early the next morning she went into the garden, calling hopelessly: "Pippin—Pippin!"

"Who—*me*?" With two squeaks, the little rascal darted from cover of a bush, ran up to her before scampering off again. He returned to her call three times that day, and once the next. Never again.

The district was renowned for weasels, so it must be assumed, and happily, that Pippin the weasel had made his own inevitable choice. By now he will have sired some very intelligent and well-informed weasels.

Another regular visitor, so regular that she is now part of the family, is Susie Hubbard. She lives with her kind mistress, Mrs. Hubbard, in a cupboard facing the loveliest part of the Dovey Valley.

To reach Mrs. Hubbard's cupboard, a distance of just over a mile from Pant Glas, means a cross-country walk through one of the most beautiful spots in Wales. Beyond my writing-room is the Pant Glas Forest, which lends about seven hundred acres of added privacy to my own domain.

From the top path and glimpsed through trees is Aberdovey, on the far side of the estuary mouth. Its white houses, reflected in the harbour, appear as dazzling teeth revealed by a friendly smile.

Descending to a lower path the integral charm of the Dovey Valley is seen in all its quiet splendour. It is an ever changing scene. Although ravines, mountains and valleys, with their subtle contours and colours, must be static, it does not seem to be so.

Throughout the seasons, by sun or moonlight, it is no penance to stroll along that path, crossing the final undulating land of the Pant gôch Wood, to call on Mother Hubbard.

Her neat bungalow seems to be one yard square! It resounds with vigorous greetings as Susie rushes out to meet the Pant Glas pack.

Such excursions are frequent, because Mother Hubbard, true to her name, is a great animal lover. We met her through Nada's puppy who found such a good home in Wales. My animals didn't lose a second in acclaiming her one of us.

Since then if something goes very wrong or very right, we telephone Mother Hubbard and up she comes.

"Come on," I say to the dogs. "We're going to meet Mother Hubbard and Susie." It's a signal for mad scampering through the forest with that purpose plainly in mind.

A streak of black rushes to meet us. More often than not mine give a perfunctory welcome to Susie before leaping forward to greet her owner, whose total height of five feet seems inadequate to meet such an onslaught.

There is nothing inadequate about Mother Hubbard. If she goes away for a few days, we look after Susie for her. If I go away, poor Mother Hubbard looks after the various needs of a minimum of forty-five animals.

Susie replaced one aged black Judy, whose devotion for twelve years had seen Mother Hubbard through sad and lonely times. Judy died and I urged a quick successor.

Susie arrived from Yorkshire, a black labrador crossed either by a sheep-dog or daddy-long-legs; we've never decided which. She has an attractive white chest. Her coat is smooth; her early days were not.

In such a small dwelling Mother Hubbard wanted a small dog. That is what she had, at first. An adorable puppy, Susie was brow-beaten by Snip who towered over her. The retrievers took it in turn to chastise or rush to Susie's help as occasion demanded.

In a matter of weeks Snip was able to walk under Susie, leaving inches to spare. Snip's manner accordingly grew less belligerent.

Nada, who had trained so many puppies in her time, shook her head sorrowfully as she regarded Susie, who would not sit or come to order.

Then Bracken took over, with no more success. She tried to show Susie how to pick up a stick in the middle before returning it to the feet of the thrower. Susie just lay on her back, laughing hysterically, before bounding off on some entirely different quest.

At last Sheena, who bears an entirely responsible outlook on life, was delegated by the others and me to see what *she* could do. Susie merely embarrassed her. When I called, Sheena came to heel, sat, fetched, carried and waited. There is nothing she enjoys better than obeying a command. Not so with Susie.

For the first ten months Susie almost wore out our vocal cords and patience. She was controlled and given some freedom; she was controlled without freedom. She was entirely controlled; she was entirely free. All the methods I knew of or could devise were applied.

"It's no good," I sighed to Mother Hubbard. "It's the daddy-long-legs in her fighting the labrador. She wants to please us, but must go hopping off at the last moment."

We had trained her to herds and flocks at the earliest possible age; at least, the goats and Jane had done so.

She had no vices. Happily, chasing and killing were of no interest. But she just liked to come home in her time, not ours. Since no dog should roam unminded in sheep country, her owner and I wasted many exasperating hours.

At last came the day when everyone's patience was exhausted. A train had been missed through having to wait upon Susie's pleasure. She had run off into the forest with a new shoe which was never found. Mother Hubbard, not in her first youth, was looking exhausted.

For days Susie had received no special scolding; only kind words, good treatment and extreme tolerance. Her fate had been discussed, but not with her.

She was to be exchanged for a clumber spaniel who must have a very kind home, but did not lean towards much exercise. Susie would be a splendid companion for a young girl who rode a great deal. Susie, well used to horses, could go out with them.

The clumber spaniel was expected early in the afternoon. Susie spent that morning curled in her favourite armchair at home, watching her mistress closely. Occasionally she would extend a paw. There was a painful crease of brow over her right eye.

Shortly after two o'clock the spaniel's owner knocked on the door. He had called to explain to Mother Hubbard that he must withdraw from the arrangement; he and his family couldn't bear to part with their old pet.

Mother Hubbard received the news almost as joyfully as Susie, who beat a steady tattoo with her tail for a long time after the visitor had gone. The thought of parting with the source of so much trouble was far worse than the trouble itself.

Susie's mistress telephoned the news to me. We were both so relieved that the impish black one must remain to madden us that our chorused statement: "Yes, well—there it is. We shall have to think of something else," carried no genuine threat.

Two days later the pack and I went to meet Mother Hubbard and Susie. I called Susie. She came, sitting at my feet. Her mistress called her and she rushed to hers. She was exemplary in all that mattered and, most strangely, had been so for forty-eight hours. From that day, when her fate nearly took a different course, she has been trainable, and anxious to learn and please.

We have discovered that Susie eavesdrops, to good purpose, although the adage about eavesdroppers is not confounded. We try her out by saying, in a light conversational tone: "She's been very good today. She came as soon as I called her." She, who has been unnamed, beats the floor furiously with her pipe-line tail. "I wonder if they would like milk now," sends Susie, not my dogs, to a cupboard where their dishes are kept.

We remind ourselves that a cross-bred dog has to contend with two forces of character. Depending upon how they are crossed, the ancestral element is apt to tug in opposite directions. Twice or thrice crossed, the struggle is greater. A good, honest mongrel, that is, one which has been crossed so many times that all trace of its origin has become submerged into one delightful creature, is unpredictable to itself as well as to its owners.

I think that what we sometimes mistakenly call "intelligence" is acute cunning. Certainly Susie has this quality to a marked degree. One can almost *hear* her arguing with herself as to the type of dog she will be on varied occasions.

I have rarely met a dog like Susie who, anxious to learn, forgets lessons so quickly. It has taken eighteen months of concentrated effort to make Susie fit for society. During that time she has been absolutely lovable and sweet tempered, but wholly exasperating.

Now Susie lies on the hearth in rhapsodic contentment with China on her chest; a study in black and white. Susie's great passion is cats.

When Chita had kittens we were anxious because of the intense interest displayed by Sheena and Susie. They were only ten days old when Sheena proudly carried a kitten from its basket, laying it at my feet. Susie did the same with another, but instead of presenting it to me she kept it between her paws while she licked it tenderly.

I was about to rush forward to return the kittens to a harassed mother, when Chita yawned, left the other kittens and walked out of doors. She was away for about a quarter of an hour, during which time I had returned the kittens to their basket, telling both dogs not to touch them.

When Chita came back she went first to Susie and then to Sheena, rubbing affectionately against each chest and purring loudly. Then she settled amongst her family.

Later I noticed that whenever Nada, Bracken or Snip approached, Chita's eyes widened; their blue was intensified. Sitting bolt upright, she was obviously on guard. But the moment Sheena or Susie appeared she relaxed, purring hopefully. More often than not she would leave both in charge while she went out for a few minutes.

I have never been able to explain that attitude on the part of Chita, who is a devoted and clever mother. Why should she trust so implicitly the only two who have never been mothers? It seemed especially odd in view of the fact that Snip actually fed the kittens for a short time in their earliest days.

But there's no knowing about cats and their mysterious ways. Take Michael, who always seems stolidly to mind his own business. He wouldn't dream of rushing forward to greet and purr round human legs, even mine.

On rare occasions when he does so I am at once wary. One summer evening two years ago he stalked from the barn to greet me with: "Er-reeow!" It was such an unusual attitude that I made a special fuss of him. He repeated his cry several times and sprang towards the knoll.

Delighted to see him so kittenish in his fourteenth year, I watched him climbing uphill before I moved away. Instantly he was back at my feet. "Er-reeow!"

"Yes, of course I'll take you a walk. But don't go that way, Michael. You'll meet the goats coming down."

When the goats take their final plunge downhill after an intoxicating day, it's no place for an ancient cat to take an evening stroll. Hoofs stab the earth with giddy abandon, horns clash like swords, drunken and unpredictable routes are taken on their merry way to bed.

That evening Simone darted under Niall's beard to avoid a playful thrust from Bambi who, thwarted, crashed into Gazelle's ribs. Gazelle's white baby, Sylvan, jumped on Bambi's back, wobbled, bleating to her mother who promptly knocked her off. Jane trotted peacefully in their wake. Evidently Belinda had gone to bed early with her three-day-old triplets.

So I guided Michael away from such an onslaught and went in the opposite direction, thinking that Michael was only playing at being a giddy goat. He didn't want to walk with me at all. I turned towards the house.

"Er-reeow!"

"You funny chap. What *is* it, Michael?"

He said it again, darted a few steps and looked back at me with singular purpose. Instead of taking him for a walk, he took me. Although he went this time past the barn into an open field, he bore left and we approached the knoll from a different direction. He must have something to show me up there, although I had never known him to act in such a manner.

Every now and then he would run back to rub against my legs, giving the same cry, before going on and up again. At the top I stopped to listen to a thin, pathetic sound. It was followed by a stronger: "Mer-air-er-aair!"

I saw Belinda's brown form pressed against the boundary fence. I could see, as she moved towards me, that her horns were not caught in the fence, as I had suspected. Then the mystery was solved.

"Oh, my poor Belinda! How long have they been there?"

"M-aair!"

I believed her. Her triplets were fast asleep — on the wrong side of the fence. They had found a small gap which had not included their mother, but must have wandered away from it. Hence their plight.

139

I handed them one by one to Belinda, who bleated gratefully. Then I turned round to tell Michael that he was a clever cat.

He had already reached the lower path and was heading for home, in the manner of a tired man who has concluded a satisfactory business deal after much effort.

I was intrigued, after I had helped Belinda to get her family home, to see Niall's beard tickling Michael's back as he rubbed against her legs. Did that cat, I wondered, run her errands for her? Never had I seen them in communication before.

But who knows how they communicate, and when? Undoubtedly in this large and growing family there are leaders and sages. I have no idea who and what defines such status, except that it is an arrangement entirely separate from human management and interference. It doesn't seem to be a question of age, strength or size.

I have a theory, which can only remain a theory, about their major activities being entirely cat-controlled. It is based on intent watching and the knowledge that Nature has some quite contrary laws. A poison as an antidote, a sting to soothe, cold to warm and death for life—as the vultures know—are a few facts which guide me. Why not an enemy as closest friend?

It seems that much of cat wisdom which is not innate stems from the birds. It's amazing how near to a watching cat a bird will come without meeting disaster.

Certainly a cat will wriggle its quarters, lash its tail and spring at the right moment, often to kill its prey. A bird provides the ultimate joy of sustained motion—of palpitating warmth.

But at Pant Glas, where numerous wild birds of many

varieties linger on the ground, we have remarkably few bird fatalities. This could be that there is constant and varied entertainment for cats in such surroundings.

Boredom could explain much of cats' so-called cruelty to birds especially. There are many animal lovers who, through circumstances, have to inflict long periods of boredom on creatures in their care. Time spent in confinement, especially if solitary, is a very long time indeed to an animal.

This is especially so in towns and suburbs, where birds, hopping on small lawns or paved terraces, provide the only mobile entertainment for a watching cat.

Cats are avid for news, whether they keep it to themselves or not. And birds have much to tell. They have the best eyesight in the world. A buzzard or falcon will see its prey on the ground from well over three thousand feet. That is why, when I let young chickens out of their safely wired enclosure, although with their mothers, I see that at least Michael, China or both are in attendance.

The mother hens seem to approve of this chaperonage. They will lurch against or peck round a watching cat, with no embarrassment to either.

When Michael gets bored with such effort, China doubles his. I often see that white cat walk towards a pair of ravens to within almost touching distance. He will *not* have them with the poultry, but he certainly doesn't try to catch or harm them.

I have never made any effort to train my cats in this respect. I don't think mine are paragons of any particular virtue; they are just very busy cats.

For instance, Michael has spent the greater part of the past ten days watching a broody hen in the barn. As soon as I close her pen at night he relaxes his self-imposed vigil. He won't hurt the hen, or the chickens when they arrive. Certainly nothing else will hurt them while he's around.

I play quite a small part in the team-spirit here. Feeding, milking and exercising dogs naturally falls to me. But I certainly haven't time to entertain or guard them individually. Happily there is no need for that. They are all so busy with each other's concerns.

If any one of them is hurt I am at once sought. They come to me of their own accord usually, or they are pushed.

A few weeks ago three clucking hens brought Pewter to me. Fanny, of course, was one of them. He was hobbling badly. I took him in the house and bathed a damaged foot. Someone, possibly Siriol, had stepped on the reigning cock. He adored the attention and for five consecutive days allowed me to bathe his injury until it was no more.

But I get my own back. I *tell* them things.

The old country superstition of *telling the bees* must have been based on profound respect for the intelligence and integrity of bees. We have only to study Maeterlinck to feel that such respect is fully justified.

So I consult my animals in all emergencies, trivial and otherwise. Do they listen? No, not they. The cats go on sleeping or washing their faces.

The dogs, especially Nada, look and look, wondering what next I shall be doing. The horses graze or stare into space, impervious to my remarks. The goats do appear to listen, but that's their way.

The poultry certainly listen when I speak, each head slightly tilted; possibly because to them it is a peculiar sound.

142

The wild birds do stay around and listen. But it's easy to seem intelligent when there is such a speedy get-away.

And yet—the word goes round. In fact, long before I have spoken, some vibration has passed from me to them, and a need is known.

It is remarkably effective.

Chapter Ten

ONE day I came out of the sea, escorted by Nada, Bracken and Sheena. We were greeted by Snip, who bounces up and down in noisy protest whenever the retrievers bathe without her.

The swim had followed a tremendous beach-combing expedition on the part of the dogs; a treasured occupation.

When we climb over the sand-dunes at Ynyslas to join the three-mile stretch of sandy beach between Borth and the Dovey estuary, the fun begins.

The dogs scatter in four directions, meeting in a streaked line when gulls lure them. This is safe sport, for the gulls are never caught. The dogs are thoroughly washed by the time they join me.

Oyster-catchers are a menace, although delightful to watch. I had heard that they are not a good combination with dogs and wondered why these small sea-birds should be in greater danger than others. I soon learned from experience that they are not. But the dogs can be severely endangered.

Like the gulls, oyster-catchers swoop down in numbers to taunt then, rising, they look like flying sardines as the sun catches their distant and retreating formations.

Within seconds they are back again. Lower, lower; to touch the dogs' heads it seems. Actually there are inches to spare. Up, up again and on, drawing the hunters towards the estuary. Sometimes the dogs are encouraged to double back, but only for a short distance. The longer spurts are always eastward towards the dreaded gap between this side and the Aberdovey beach.

When first I realized what was happening I called and called, with no effect. The dogs were hunting flat out and had no ears for me.

At ebb tide this sport on the part of oyster-catchers is played at full energy. When the tide is rushing in or is high there is little point in their efforts, for the dogs would be balked by water and might stop to think.

What appears to be a stretch of wet sand followed by a line of clear water, almost jumping width, is not so. The estuary is extremely dangerous to cross without expert knowledge.

Watching my dear ones being lured to the brink of that glistening streak, so near to Aberdovey, I knew real fear. As many human swimmers had made fatal attempts to cross from one shore to the other, why should the dogs not be swept or dragged by dangerous currents?

I ran as fast and as far as I could. Then, horrified, I watched the sinister play of bird with dog, of tide with sand.

At last I saw Snip's white body, appearing as a tiny spot, on the farthest point of coast beyond Aberdovey. Then bodies, the colour of sand, seemed to move in the sand beside her. It would mean a twenty-mile journey by road to fetch the truants—if they lived that long. For the tide had turned.

Waiting ten minutes, which seemed like two hours, I was rewarded at last. Sheena's sense of responsibility must have revived. She was headed towards me. With relief, I watched her coming from the distant and receding sand-bar. She had been sitting beside me for ten minutes before the others, still specks on the horizon, turned towards us.

My wordy reproofs were lost as they gathered round, only to start barking wildly again when the oyster-catchers returned to lure them.

"No!"

It had effect, if not immediately. Snip, who was last to relent, came to me sideways, as she always does when guilty.

Then I strode out quickly for Borth, where I met a friend, Myra, who lived at the foot of Pant Glas. Having found some-one to mind my clothes, to save Snip dragging them to me at the water's edge, I went for a delicious swim.

Nada makes a comforting "hot-water bottle" in deep water. She swims alongside for as far as I care to go, then is pleased when I give her a rest in my arms. On occasions I lend her to a stranger who is looking blue and shivery. Over sixty pounds of solid golden retriever is an astonishing but warming article to borrow in deep water.

It takes time to convince Bracken and Sheena that we're not drowning. Once their cries for help on our behalf have died down they join us. We swim back in line, I keeping well away from sharp claws. In a rough sea it's great fun, because the dogs frequently mislay me on the crest of a wave. They are still scrabbling about in foam when I drift safely into shallow water to laugh at their efforts.

On that particular day, when the water was nearly as warm as the atmosphere, the sea was like a sheet of glass. Myra and I lingered in the evening sunshine before piling wet and tired dogs into the back of the Land-Rover.

From the beach at Borth it is possible to look inland and see a white gable end of Pant Glas peeping through the wooded hills two miles inland; three miles by road.

"It's so still and peaceful," Myra breathed. "You can just see . . ." She stopped, gasping. My glance towards the Pant Glas woods followed hers.

We exchanged looks, so appalled, that the need of speech was dismissed.

We rushed to the Land-Rover, bundling the dogs in. I put my foot down on the accelerator. We had wobbled precariously round several bends before we both uttered together:

"I'm afraid it's my house."

As one of us must be most blessedly wrong, we laughed; a thin but welcome sound.

"That spiral of smoke's coming from Pant Glas," I insisted.

"I don't think so. It's coming from mine. Smoke rises."

"Not on such a still night." I added gloomily that my mother must have knocked over a kerosene stove.

She said that it was far more likely to be the result of her husband's pipe left in the wrong place—burning.

"Burning" was the key word. For certainly something in the Pant Glas area was burning well. We each indulged our separate and horrific ideas silently, trying to comfort the other by saying, in chorus: "It's certainly my house, not yours."

We swept into the village, to be assured that Myra's house was intact. Fire engines were approaching but I didn't stay to ask questions.

Never had my own drive seemed longer. I pictured my mother unconscious and animals trapped in rooms or sheds, as the pungent fumes reached me.

But as I leapt out, racing towards the home terrace, I knew that the cottage and surroundings were, strangely, untouched.

My mother met me with a placid smile. "You're always in such a hurry, dear. It's too warm for you to be racing about like this."

I said something, rushed to the forest gate and saw smoke belching through and over the trees. Myra and I made simultaneous efforts to telephone each other, so jamming the line. When at last she was through she told me: "There's a great fire in the forest between us. I'll give the firemen tea down here, if you'll see to the men at your end."

Once I knew that the fire was in the hands of competent foresters and firemen I relaxed. But we all remained conscious of the fact that the natural fire breaks between the forest and my beloved home and inmates were too narrow for safety. At eight o'clock in the evening it wanted only the slightest breeze to fan the whole danger into startling reality.

Until well after midnight we were supplying a dozen or more tired, grimy and hungry men with substantial snacks and tea. At two o'clock we were told that the danger had passed.

Once more I was struck by the innate courtesy of the local people. Not only did all those foresters and firemen call within two days, to thank us for hospitality, but the officer in command of the Fire Brigade paid a personal visit with the same purpose in mind. We had a charming letter from the Forestry Commission. In fact everyone thanked us heartily for letting them save our home, possibly our lives, after so much hard work on their part!

Coming from the raw Midlands, I found such an attitude refreshing.

No sooner had mutual thanks been returned than trouble flared again. This time a serious situation was saved by my young goat, Simon.

Simon and Simone were Niall's twins. Simone is here still, but in that hot summer of many accidental fires, Simon was allowed his first three months of delirious happiness before other arrangements had to be made for him. That is always a worrying state of affairs, because male goats can have such a thin time if they fall into casual hands.

He was particularly fortunate. A local squire, the owner of several thousand acres, thought that Simon would be ideal as a pet. So he proved to be—for a time. Eventually his master did the right thing by Simon, taking endless trouble to pass him into other kind keeping, where rose gardens wouldn't tempt him.

Simon's lot was an exception. I usually find it far kinder to have male goats put down by the vet at birth. Malpas has proved a profitable exception to that rule.

Three days after the fire Simon was eagerly awaited at his new home. My mother and I took him in the Land-Rover. He settled comfortably in her lap, intent on enjoying every moment of his new experience. Even the jolting on our only path to the village caused him no concern.

If it hadn't been for Simon I should not have had occasion to drive that day. So I should not have glanced at the bright green of our larches to exclaim, not on their beauty but—"Oh—oh dear!"

A thin, blue spiral rose beyond the larches, which meant— fire in the Pant Glas woods again.

It was Saturday and few people were about. There were no

foresters on duty. Those who were on fire-watching guard had larger areas in mind. It was a bad summer for fires. Broken bottles, cigarette ends and other careless tokens of town visitors in such weather take their inevitable toll.

A mile or so ahead I raised the alarm and drove on to deliver Simon. While at his new home I had a message from Myra: "I think you'd better come home. The fire engines have just arrived."

So the work started all over again. There was no week-end rest for foresters or firemen. This time the fire took much getting under control; the whole week-end.

If I hadn't given the alarm when I had, vast damage would have been done. My animals would have been left without shelter; so should we.

In due course we all started to thank each other again. I didn't forget to go to Niall on the same mission.

"If it hadn't been for your son, old lady, we should all have been living in one large bell tent by now."

"Tee-hee-hee—maair!"

I didn't agree with her. I told her that at times her sense of humour was misplaced. I had forgotten her addiction: smoke in any form is an exquisite pleasure to Niall, as to many goats.

So for the better part of a week those goats were in their seventh heaven. They bumped into each other in their absurd and newly acquired habit of wandering about with raised heads. They wore what I called their "Ah, Bisto!" look.

The aroma lingered for days; so did the goats' leering expressions. Eyes half closed, the tip of her beard thrust skywards and top lip raised in approval, Niall's attitude, in particular, to the forest fire was one of deepest appreciation.

When at last it was possible to walk in the forest without tears streaming down my face, caused by smouldering undergrowth, I realized that at least the goats looked bereft. So I decided to cheer them with a special treat; a private bonfire. That never fails to thrill them.

Whenever I go out with armfuls of rubbish, kerosene and matches, the air is tense with expectancy. The goats hang about, and when the last red embers have faded they paw the ashes to revive the glorious smell.

If the ashes remain hot, or look as if they might be, Gazelle is gently nosed forward to sit on the remains of the fire. If she doesn't get up hastily, or bleat in pain, then she is hurried off by Niall, who takes precedence.

After ten minutes or so of happily rocking to and fro in the warm ashes, Niall relinquishes her place to one of her grown daughters. They sit for a time before passing on such delectation to their children.

By the time Gazelle's turn comes round, there's nothing worth sitting in for her or her daughter, Sylvan.

But Sylvan will surprise those goats one day. Already she towers over the rest and is a maiden milker. She is hornless and has a sweet disposition, coupled with a quiet determination. She might have learned of her mother's early days with the herd, when she was battered about because she was not of The Blood, and was a house pet.

I don't know at what age Niall will pass on her leadership or to whom. I suppose that her own health and vigour will govern her decision. But as my animals are noted for their exceptionally long lives, we needn't bother about that just yet.

I am sure that when the day comes for a new leader to take

over, the ceremony will be worth watching. The position might be taken up gradually, for there is much to learn.

The appointment doesn't merely consist of being leader of the goat train. There is profound knowledge of herb lore to be passed to each growing member of the herd—at discretion.

Happily Pant Glas is without rhododendrons. But I had not been here long before someone kindly gave me one plant, which I set in the garden.

Rhododendrons are a potent poison to many animals, especially to goats. Not knowing of their danger, I was unperturbed when the goats trespassed in the garden. Gazelle had been with the herd then for a month or so, and seemed to be still on probation. She had not yet presented them with Sylvan.

I remained unruffled as I watched the herd ravish the garden, knowing it would have many more nettles and weeds to offer than valued plants. It was an easy and comprehensive way of preparing the land for human efforts later.

I actually saw Niall eyeing Gazelle who was enjoying a tasty morsel. Minutes later Belinda went to the same spot and Niall, who had remained near by, took a flying crash with her head at Belinda's ribs. The attack seemed entirely uncalled for, and my sympathies were with the surprised daughter.

Presently Bambi went to the spot, where Gazelle had nibbled undisturbed. She received the same treatment. I told Niall that I thought her behaviour mean and unnecessary. She gave me a bland stare and went her own way.

The next day Gazelle was violently ill. After a distressing morning I realized that her symptoms were those of poisoning, and acted accordingly. I had to get veterinary help. Having spent the better part of two nights with her in the stable, I was relieved that Gazelle slowly revived.

The vet said that it seemed to be rhododendron poisoning, but I assured him that there were none on the premises. Suddenly I remembered the plant which I had set in the garden.

I hurried to inspect and there, sure enough, was a nibbled plant of that offending species, which I rooted up and burnt.

It was the identical spot where Gazelle had lingered with such disastrous result—calmly watched by Niall.

I recalled how Niall had thrust her daughters from the danger. But Gazelle, the interloper, she had watched with malignant contempt. I suppose she decided that Gazelle should learn such truths the hard way. I'm afraid goats are like that.

But let one of the herd, which happily now includes Gazelle and Sylvan, be in danger, then no one is quicker than the leader to fetch help or take completely sane and remedial action.

Ivy leaves have great toning-up qualities and are greatly relished by all goats, especially after kidding. In fact I have often been nudged along by Niall towards a favoured spot. There I reach up, gather and distribute ivy leaves. I happen to know that the berries are severe poison to them, which fact Niall must have noted and approved. I do believe that if I foolishly gathered ivy berries, offering them to any member of the herd, I should soon feel the shock of her iron-hard head in my solar plexus.

In fact, when an ivy-covered tree crashed to the ground in a gale I mistakenly thought that the goats would have a wonderful time. Three of them did.

Niall, unable to cope with young and foolish goats coming from all directions, delegated the horned Belinda and Bambi to work with her.

As soon as a youngster approached the tempting ivy, it was attacked by its nearest and dearest in no uncertain manner. Niall, having no horns, made full use of her teeth. It's surprising how effective a goat bite can be, considering that they each have only a bottom row of teeth.

After ears had been nipped, ribs and flanks cruelly charged, the uninitiated gave up in favour of safer grazing. Only when the herd had dispersed did Niall and her elder daughters gorge at will on the ivy leaves.

When I realized what was happening and that there were far too many berries to pick by hand, I turned the fallen tree to better use. Burning and crackling, it fully compensated all who had been so ruthlessly thrust aside.

There are occasions in most days, especially when sun floods the valley from dawn until sunset, when joy of living and exuberant spirits take vocal form. Often this is mid-morning or in the early afternoon, preceding a siesta.

The peace of Pant Glas is constant. Bird song, the faint rustle of leaves, perpetual melody from the brook, the distant bleating of sheep and scores of fainter sounds are so interwoven with silence as to be mistaken for it.

Suddenly the attuned ear can be startled by a different note: "Cluk-cluk" or "Mair-er-aair" in the immediate vicinity.

It is often a signal that gossip is about to take place, especially if Siriol has mislaid Bess and calls out to ask where he left her.

Somebody else decides that they have also lost a friend. A busybody points out that if they'd been paying attention such confusion need not have been. Then everyone speaks at once, possibly meaning: "She's over here," "He's over there," "She's laying in the lay."

The actual sounds are less distinct but, in chorus, hearty:

"Wherr-err-wherr-err-wherr," sings Siriol.

"Cluk,cluk-wherk."

"Mair-er-aair."

"Mer." Jane, with briefest diaologue, brings much wool with her at a gallop to see what's to do.

"Hmmmmmmmmmm." Bess's tactful reminder comes in a gentle contralto tone.

"Ell-ow." Chita's very fond of mingling with a throng of legs. The astonishing thing is that she never gets trodden on.

It's too much for the dogs, who have been dreaming on the terrace. "Snap," says Snip. The retrievers have mellow voices but of great volume. Susie Hubbard has such a deep bark as to make her sleek black form seem inadequate; only a wolfhound or mastiff is entitled to the sound.

"Quiet, dogs—quiet!" An unfair injunction in the circumstances and unheeded. The dogs become quiet in their own time and long before their friends beyond the gate.

To an "Uk-uk-wherk" and an "Oodle-doodle-doo", Pewter adds his: "Ah-doodle-ah-doodle-ah-doodle-oodle-oo", which should settle matters for the poultry. Not a bit of it.

Then Bambi pushes her horns over the gate, wearing her "Bread for the love of Allah" look. That is actually what she seeks as she moans: "Mair-uh-maaair!" Bread is often taken to her when she has repeated the forlorn cry too often.

Jane has a head-pressing match with the young goat, Melody. The smallest goat here and, surely, the widest sheep in the world seem unequally matched. I suspect their efforts are stalemate only because of Jane's kind nature. When she takes on a goat of Bambi's colossal size Jane is rarely out-butted.

She has found that slightly different measures are needed if she is to hold her own with goats. This head-crashing business seems to be much on a par with human cronies who, in bursts of arch enthusiasm, accompany a loud guffaw by clamping a hand on another's shoulder.

Crash! The animals are more graceful than we could hope to be. The goats dance on their hind legs and then they crash. Horns to the hornless, or in matching pairs, no harm is done.

As excitement grows and, possibly, slightly bawdy tales are exchanged, these social crashes have an almost frightening quality to a new observer.

But far from rendering each other unconscious, fresh vigour is gained and mounts, to reach a frenzied peak but for the regular introduction of an anti-climax.

As two of these monsters, for indeed they seem to be so in the perpendicular, are about to descend again, a hen runs fast between them: "Uk-uk-wherk-wherk." It could mean: "Excuse me, I've somewhere to go, quickly." Or the white cat, without a trace of fear, rolls nonchalantly on his back, apparently with suicidal intent.

It is strange that no large creature here ever hurts a small one. They will change direction in mid air rather than trample, as a horse will avoid a fallen rider.

So, having been interrupted, one or both forget what they were about and turn away to loll or graze.

What Jane lacks in agility and height, for she never demeans herself by strutting about on two legs like a human, she must make up for with a cast-iron neck and spine. Her shock resistance is abnormal.

She will receive and return the first plunge of a head against her own with minimum movement. Before the next attack she bustles back two steps. As the game hots up and her opponent dances at full height before crashing, Jane retreats five or six steps, so gaining full impetus before jerking forward to—*sock*.

She has never lost a round yet. As no one ever seems the worse for this peculiar game, it could be stated that Jane is the winner. She certainly "gives as good as she gets" and at all times her manner is unobtrusive but never cringing. So she has won lasting respect from all the goats.

Once respect is lost between animals it seems a hopeless task to bring them together peaceably. We have only one such case here due, I fear, to a slight inferiority complex in the first instance.

When I added the white kitten, China, to the family, the resident cats, Michael and Panda, accepted him with a couple of spits, followed by rubbing, purring and, eventually, friendship. The three forgathered at meal times in a row. They sunned and slept together on occasions.

From the start China adored every living creature on the premises. He is not only representative of the wonderful *camaraderie* which the animals have established, but he greatly adds to that spirit with a benevolence all his own.

So when Chita, the seal-point Siamese, joined us I had no qualms. That dainty, affable little person, with her extraordinary voice, enchanted all who met her. Even Snip's early protests were overcome when Chita, ignoring the dangerously raised lip, curled up on Snip's tummy and went to sleep.

There has always been a regal quality to Chita. Her undeniable breeding and charm are quietly there; she has no need to stress them. She notices animals and people, remembers their names and where they usually sit or stand. I suspect that, in her own language, she uses the royal "We".

When she first said: "Ell-ow!" to the cats and ran up the curtains, she must have meant: "Now we will play."

When or how the feud began I'm not at all certain. One day she was chasing, and being chased by Panda in friendly abandon. The next day Panda's "Ptssz!" sounded genuine.

At last I came to understand that whenever Panda met Chita there was a petrified silence, until Panda said "Ptssz!" and vanished for the day.

Chita began to look for Panda. As soon as she sighted her, the dark brown tail lashed so furiously that the cat was almost waved.

Then came the awful occasion when the queen of Siam swore. I heard it myself; it did happen. Not "We are not amused." Nothing as harmless as that. The sound came from the very depths of Chita:

"Er-blery-ow-amews!"

And she uttered it in public, too. Poor Panda grew to twice her size. Although she remained black and white, I'm sure she was scarlet inside.

She retreated. I will say that for Panda. And she has done so ever since. She never adopts the cheapening attitude of: "I'm as good as you are." When in the royal presence she absents herself backwards, and then runs as if the Devil himself were after her.

For weeks after that all we saw of Panda, when Chita was about, was one large green eye pressed to the crack of a doorway or staring through leaves high in a tree.

As far as I know Chita has never attacked Panda. But she takes malicious delight in approaching her sideways, turning on the full power of her brilliant eyes which glow with ruby behind the sapphire, and then she curses: "Er-blery-ow-amews!" Panda's terrified squawk gives her keen satisfaction.

This slight rift in an otherwise perfectly harmonious family circle is a nuisance. It means furtive tiptoeing round the premises at dusk, accompanied by the whispered: "Come along, Panda. Chita's not here." Doors and windows are slammed or opened at inconvenient times to protect Panda — not from terrible assault, but from gross insults.

Gradually Panda had the wit to know that there are three long periods in each year when Chita is in "a condition". Through the last five weeks of each pregnancy and the subsequent seven or eight weeks when kittens are all-absorbing, Panda goes about unscared and unoffended.

I have an awful suspicion that it is Panda who hustles up some quite unsuitable tom cat from the village, procuring him with seductive sounds and promises.

Chapter Eleven

SOMETIMES on a summer evening, when the sun is passing day into the safe keeping of a pale moon, the social life of Pant Glas begins.

Since the cottage was enlarged a simple terrace has been added. Below this the ground slopes some distance to a talkative brook. The whole area of about a quarter of an acre is fenced, with gates at either end of the terrace.

This makes a pleasant spot for sun-bathing. Friends who come from a distance suspiciously, for—*two or three days*, are apt, on their third consecutive week at Pant Glas, to loll on the terrace, giving me the benefit of sound and accumulated advice.

"So wise of you, dear, to have put a good fence round the house. It does keep the animals away. It's a pity the stables are so near, don't you think?"

I point out that the cottage has spread outwards to meet the stables. "In fact, the dining-room was a stable."

A deep sigh of contentment is often followed by a shorter sigh of different calibre. Here it comes!

"Such an ideal spot for a writer! Of course, I can't *think* how you ever manage to write a word with all these animals about. Now, don't you think if you lessened them—cut them by half—you'd find much more time for writing?"

At that point I take pleasure in pointing out that I've written and sold more than a dozen novels in less than five years. This often brings forth the odd comment: "I know, but you won't go on at that rate for ever. Something will break."

I shudder. It seems polite to shudder at times. If the advice and terrible predictions go on at length, to avoid laughing in the wrong place I make an excuse:

"I must give Chita her tablet."

"There you are! What does a healthy cat want medicine for?"

"Not medicine exactly. Osteocalcium will help her kittens."

"Help them? Surely you won't *keep* them?"

"No, they'll all find good homes at the right time. I just like to make sure of their bone formation being as perfect as possible. It helps Chita, too."

"I think you ought to drown all but one. Don't think I'm interfering. It's none of my business, but . . ."

"Ger-row!"

"Oh, here you are, Chita! Come on—your tablet."

Chita knows where the tablets are kept. When she has submitted to treatment we exchange whispered confidences:

"All but one kitten, Chita—eh?"

"Ger-row!"

"*No*, darling," I say firmly, knowing that if Chita had more worldly knowledge she would have suggested: "Bradshaw on breakfast table," not: "Ger-row!" I don't waste words on her, explaining the rudiments of hospitality.

When visitors tire of blaming the animals for something which will mysteriously break, and so far hasn't, invariably they advise me on sounder lines:

"I'm amazed that you have so many callers up here."—
We're only a quarter of a mile from the village.

"Yes, visitors can be distracting."

"When I've gone I hope you'll really settle down to writing."

"I write at night, after you're in bed."

"Yes, but you can't keep that up. I hope no one else is coming to stay?"

I laugh and enumerate the friends who are coming for separate *few days*, only to be told:

"I don't think it's right. You shouldn't have them. How can you entertain people and write? They must be made to understand; you write for a living."

As I have this advice from practically each friend in turn I don't listen too attentively. My glance has caught a thin line wending from the top fields to join another advancing from the knoll.

The tabby Michael, hunched on the bank opposite the stables, has been interviewed by his white friend, China, who springs on to the gate-post. He always does that when there's something to see.

Upstairs Panda has her half-Persian coat pressed closely to the window-pane. The window-seat there makes a splendid "royal box". She can't see who's coming, but knows that she will see all in due course.

The four-square sheep, Jane, trots under Bess's feet, stopping at the brook to drink with the horses. But only Siriol is there. Belle Jones hasn't looked up from luscious grazing yet. When she does, she will realize that the other two cobs have gone without her, and then . . .

The dogs are making a small pandemonium on the terrace. Nada, Sheena and Snip are pretending to kill Bracken, who loves it.

Chita, who had thought of spending the evening on a cushioned seat in the picture window with her children, changes her mind. She darts into the garden and up the damson tree. From there she decides which way the cat will jump.

The poultry are just going to bed. That's always a sight worth watching. There are sixteen hens, Pewter and Archibald. In the day-time each cockerel is followed or surrounded by eight hens. At bedtime the Pewter birds and the Archie birds are apt to get mixed. This causes terrible chaos.

Three Pewter birds will wander under the raised slat to the sleeping-quarters, followed by two Archie birds.

Pewter, who really likes to go to bed first, often has to stay to round up several late wives; so does Archibald. Nothing will induce Archibald to go indoors in line with Pewter. He learned the folly of such action months ago.

Archibald is always learning something new. I watched him having a lesson in etiquette one evening. Four of his ladies had preceded him; the other four were dotted about, picking up last minute bargains. So it seemed reasonable to me that Archibald should draw their attention to duty in a usual manner: "Ooodle-doodle-ooo!"

His mistimed call had immediate and aggravating effect. Seven Pewter birds, who had gone before their lord to the bedchamber, came scurrying out again as if it were morning.

It was too much for Pewter. With a heavy flap of his grey wings, he lumbered over to Archibald and boxed his ears. He did more than that. Poor Archibald went to bed minus several gorgeously red feathers and one bottle green from his tail.

Apparently it isn't done to Ooodle-doodle-ooo when retiring for the night. Come to think of it, I've never again heard the sound once the final trek has started. Not only was that code most sensibly established, but it also underlines the general tone of behaviour for which Pewter is such a stickler.

I find that the hour of bedtime, which encompasses so much scuffling, shoving, "Wherk-wherks" and "Uk-uk-uks", is decidedly smoother when the cat, China, is present with the poultry. He is their great friend and approved by all; possibly because he is white and they can see him easily.

Often China will sit in one of the laying-boxes, intent on mousing possibilities. The birds naturally believe that he is entranced by *them*.

At times a hen will ride into the shed on China's back. I've never met such an amiable and tolerant cat. A flurry of feathers in his face causes him no concern; he doesn't even sneeze.

When sport is high China spends the entire night with the poultry. This means that I have to take his meal to him, which he eats daintily before returning to work. Near my own bed-time I usually remember to look in, to see if China wants to be released. More often than not I find him still vigilant, or fast sleep between two hens. I imagine that these are lent to him in return for mousing labours so freely given.

But on a "social" evening China doesn't retire with the poultry. He is on his gate-post—waiting.

There is a stillness as, in ones and twos, in groups or singly, the animals saunter homewards.

Michael, still on the bank, washes his face as if he'd never washed it before.

Chita moves to the entrance steps followed by six tiny replicas of herself. Twelve coffee-coloured ears, six long coffee-coloured tails and twenty-four coffee-coloured legs pounce round her and at each other. Seven pairs of brilliant sapphires are ready to stare at the first arrivals.

"We're having a party tonight."

A guest is due to exclaim: "Really, you are absurd! Why didn't you tell me sooner? What shall I wear?"

I explain that it won't be that sort of party and there's no need to change. Glancing at the *Radio Times*, I announce: "It couldn't be better; orchestral music. They're going to play *Strauss*. Oh yes, and several good marches!"

Securing the gates leading to the forest and vegetable garden, I then throw open the main entrance gates, rejoining my own kind. There are too many gnats for us to sit outside in comfort. I explain that we shall be better on the window-seat. Our visitors will be less self-conscious if left to entertain themselves.

"Ell-low!"

Chita has gone forward to welcome Niall. The goat looks at the cat as if she were a kipper served thoughtlessly on top of a *pêche melba*. With an expression of distaste Niall shoves at Chita, but misses her. The reason is simple; Chita has stepped aside to present her six children for Niall's delight or confusion.

The kittens are rarely all together at the same time. Two of them are entranced by Niall's long beard. They reach up to tap it, falling through the silky hair into each other's paws.

Then, backs arched and tails fuzzed like hairy caterpillars, they dart away sidewards to collide with three more kittens who are about to inspect the oddity.

Niall endures this stoically, lowering her beard to the ground in solemn meditation. She ignores the sudden "Pitssz!" as the kittens meet her. One of them runs back to Chita—a quick suck for dutch courage. The other two have scattered in bewilderment.

There is always one child in a litter who is first to tumble from the maternal basket to inspect the mysteries of the new world. That one usually can be counted on for original and enterprising behaviour in most circumstances. Such a one was Pinto.

So Pinto, undaunted, goes up to Niall and squeaks: "L'ow!", pressing her wee head against the goat's hoof.

Niall, that most efficient mother, grandmother and great-grandmother many times over, is nonplussed. She knows that the young have to be dealt with, but how does one deal with —this? While she is seeking an answer from her store of wisdom, she is astounded to feel Pinto dart up her leg.

Pinto doesn't stay there long because Niall, uttering "Un-nun-nun," has shaken her back to the ground and blown her hair the wrong way. Undaunted, Pinto goes back for more, purring with delight. She likes Niall.

So Niall does what she should have done in the first place— she smells out the texture of Pinto, beginning at the base of the tail and working along the spine.

Whatever she gleans from such minute inspection must be amusing. Head thrown right back, Niall curls her top lip to show her one row of teeth. She chortles, shakes and bursts out laughing. She is still "Tee-hee-heeing" as she goes slowly down the slope where many fine and rare herbs grow.

Pinto, deciding that Niall can take a joke and is, in fact, the largest joke she has met in her four and a half weeks on earth, goes with her. The large British Saarnen goat and the microscopic Siamese are a quaint combination as they plunge downhill together, intent on making the most of Pinto's first party. Chita, unalarmed, turns her sapphires towards the next arrivals.

The brown, horned Belinda trips along. She is always graceful and gives the impression of wearing high heels. She is an elegant matron. Surrounded by her goatling triplets, she hustles them along in case the gates should close. Her colouring is effectively broken by pale gold markings in symmetrical lines on either side of her nose. These are matched by her drooping ears.

The triplets cavort on the terrace before sampling the entrance steps to the house. They are delighted to see Nada coming forward to have a word with them.

The other two retrievers are ready to mingle, but Snip is restrained by human hands until she becomes more sociable.

Then Belinda's twin comes hurrying along with her two children. Looking hopefully at the window, Bambi gives her mournful cry: "Mair-uh-maaair!" She only thinks in terms of bread. As soon as she knows that hospitality has failed, she moves off to the next best thing—a nettle bed.

A goatling who is always shy when separated from Niall, stands uncertainly in the gateway. The cat, Michael, noticing her hesitation, rubs against her and escorts her half-way down the slope towards Niall, who cries out: "Eeeya" and goes on nibbling.

There is a sound like a roll of drums. A slight earth tremor is felt as Siriol grasps the fact that something is going on. Turf and dust fly as his hoofs pound at a gallop. He arrives, skidding to a neat pause at the entrance, before bellowing to the other cobs.

Bess follows him at once, but Belle has mislaid herself again. She is probably musing in a fragrant hollow, or dreaming that she is where she isn't. There will be trouble when she finds the other two have gone to a party without her.

Close behind the horses glides a white, shapeless figure. It is a signal for China to leave his look-out post and join the ladies. "Mer!"

There is a certain amount of gush in China's greeting, as he rubs himself into Jane's wool. He has always adored Jane, who taught him the joys of head-pressing. From some aspects it is an unfortunate alliance, because the pure white form emerging through Jane's forelegs robs the sheep of her once virginal snow appearance. I wonder if I could hire the pair out to a soap manufacturer?

Siriol presses his nose flat against the window-pane. It brings forth wild staccato protests from Snip. From time to time the terrier has bared her teeth at each visitor in turn, promising them final and immediate disintegration when she is let out. No one believes her.

To prove the point I open the door and Snip hesitates. "Come and speak to them properly now, Snip."

She throws me a swift little side glance, showing much white to her eye as she takes up the challenge. Hoping that no one too large will notice her, she plops down the steps. Her stubby tail is at half-mast as enormous, hairy legs approach her.

She makes a tactful noise in her throat, which could mean nothing more pugnacious than: "Excuse me. I wasn't barking at you—naturally."

With the whole ghastly pantomime spread before and around her, Snip sidles off to smell—a flower. She smells it for a long time and would have gone on smelling indefinitely, had Bambi not chosen that very flower as an "after" to a thistle she had just eaten with relish.

Bambi's method of removing any small animal from a dish she is about to savour is peremptory. With a squeak of dismay Snip rushes down the bank to meet Niall coming up. At least Niall, unlike Bambi, is hornless. Snip falters.

She is beginning to wish that she had not hurled so many insults when glass protected her. Her remorse is visible; her resource can only be speculated on. Will she hare back to safety, or stand her ground?

The kitten, Pinto, offers a happy solution. Bounding along beside Niall, the tiny Siamese springs joyfully at Snip. In ordinary circumstances her reception might not have been so genial. But Snip is wily.

With every show of affection, maternal solicitude and friendly care, she welcomes Pinto as a long lost daughter.

Pinto is delighted. She springs at the wagging stump, misses it and darts to Snip's chest. Looking up hopefully she gets a lick on her cheek.

Although Snip noses Pinto gently, Chita doesn't trust the situation. She leaves her other kittens in Sheena's care and rushes to Pinto.

"Ger-row!"

Snip takes the order in good part because she has to. Even

169

when Pinto fastens needle-sharp teeth into her leg, she remains affable.

Chita, only relieved that her child is in good company, rolls over to show Snip her underneath. Snip duly admires the oyster shading which goes so well with dark brown, then the three come up the hill together.

Perhaps only I see the furtive glances which Snip casts over her shoulder at Niall, who apparently has forgotten her.

Where can she sit in safety? Nowhere really, but she decides to shelter beside Bracken on the boulder step. Bracken is of a nervous disposition and might need protection. She watches two late-comers arrive, but doesn't give her usual welcome.

Gazelle rolls along, looking more like a llama than a goat. With her, and towering above the rest of the herd, is Sylvan, her daughter.

The fact that Sylvan is dearly loved by the herd, and fondly tolerated by Niall, affords Gazelle intense satisfaction. Her own appealing looks faded long ago and she tends to overrate her daughter's. But what mother doesn't? She spends hours looking at Sylvan through half-closed eyes, doubtless planning a brilliant future for her.

Shaggy, and lacking the fine breeding of her companions, Gazelle hovers in the gateway, shoving her daughter gently forward with her head. There is no need for anxiety on her part for, with all the confidence in the world, Sylvan runs to Niall, nipping her playfully on the ear. They indulge a little violent butting. Gazelle, with her peculiar gait, caused by knees in and hoofs out, moves in to the party, the most contented dowager of them all.

There is plenty to watch. Although they seem to have long

periods when they graze, nose, nibble or scratch within the precincts—precious to them because it is unusual—there is always some pocket drama or tomfoolery going on somewhere.

Bambi decides to share the boulder step with Snip and Bracken. With a thin yell, Snip hares off only to find herself nudged back into position by Sylvan.

I glance at the time. "You can turn on the radio now."

The suggestion is followed by an ear-splitting yell. Why should some prima donna at her worst be singing that particular opera to the strains of a rousing march?

"One fine day I'll see you . . . Brrrh—snuck!"

My apologies to the B.B.C.! Their orchestral leader could hardly have know that Belle would choose that very moment to arouse from her dreams and find herself deserted.

The ground shakes and vibrates seconds before Belle appears, wearing, as usual, a bramble in her mane. Standing within sight of the party but not yet of it, she looks like an outsize Ophelia as her white forelock lifts in the evening breeze.

The charge, which she has halted for the purpose of summing up an unexpected situation, is continued. Head raised as she repeats her theme song, fore feet flung high and wide, she rushes to join her friends.

Although she arrives with a terrific clatter no one is unduly disturbed. They all know that, despite her weight and size, Belle Jones is essentially gentle and that the smallest member of the family is entirely safe with her.

From the awed expression of my human visitor such assurance needs confirmation. "Is it safe to have the horses in? Surely something could get hurt?"

"It could, but it won't."

To prove this four kittens pounce at Belle's hind feet. Michael says "good evening" in his way, then leads Belle down the slope towards Siriol and Bess.

Meanwhile a selection from *Merrie England* is influencing the party spirit. The horses and goats are most affected by music. Ears point towards it and in no time they are inspecting the box which produces such magical sound.

I'm pleased to say that I have only one animal who is mechanically minded. Such knowledge can become a pest.

Chita knows just what to do to the centre portion of a portable wireless set to cut off a programme instantly.

Such interference can't be ascribed to coincidence. She began by sitting on the set, possibly because it gave forth such strange and elusive purrs. The centre disc automatically swivelled round and sound faded.

She is allergic to brass instruments and some human singing voices. Who is she to complain!

On three separate occasions, when the noise has not been to her liking, milady has either sat on it or used her paw, fiddling about until the screech had gone. One day she switched from opera to a foreign station and seemed quite content to listen to an excitable discourse in French.

So if I remark to a human visitor: "Mind Chita! She'll switch off," it's not altogether surprising if I get a peculiar stare, to which I am now well used.

As at most parties, there is a lull. The guests are so absorbed in their change of environment and the delicacies it offers, they are content to eat in silence.

Jane has formed a small mountain of herself for China and

two kittens to explore. She looks at nothing in particular and sees all.

At one such party, when all likely guests were present and had reached the lull stage, an unusual form of gate-crashing took place. It was already dusk and therefore exceptional.

A remarkable sound drew the attention of all present to the entrance. It was uttered with absolute clarity and presence. What a toast-master! "Milords, ladies and gentlemen, pray silence for. . . ." It could well have meant just that.

"Ah-doodle-ah-doodle-ah-doodle-oodle-oo!"

"But the poultry went to bed ages ago!" someone exclaimed to me.

True. But they had all got up again. Pewter then had been with us for only a week or so, and such revellings had not been indulged in during his waking or sleeping presence.

Doubtless he had hopped from his perch, popped under the slat, which I had not lowered, and strutted round the corner to see what was happening.

Such *goings on* he beheld that he must have gathered his ladies, who followed him obediently. At that time Pewter reigned supreme, for Archibald the Second was a leggy youngster known only as Nearly.

"Mer!" Jane was pleased to see her day-time friends, and stood up to greet them.

In they came, mingling with the cats, dogs, kittens, horses, goats and sheep. They looked quite a colourful array as they peck-pecked at the new ground, to which I added a few discreet breadcrumbs.

They didn't stay long. Their visit was well timed for it tallied with the orchestra playing *The Grasshoppers' Dance* by

Bucalossi. It was then I realized that music means as much to poultry as to any other creature.

Little Fanny wore such a dreamy look as she trotted beside Pewter.

The arrival of the poultry livened up the whole party. Belle raced up the bank to blow hot air into Nada's coat. The goats paired off for head-crashing matches, and cats and kittens darted up trees and posts in all directions.

Chita said: "Ell-ow!" to Mrs. Henry Wood, who, squawking, rushed to Pewter for protection; doubtless declaring that she had been insulted.

One moment the poultry were very much there; the next nowhere to be seen. Pewter, like any decent, important personage, having arrived with a fanfare of trumpets, absented himself and entourage as unobtrusively as possible.

I went quietly to the poultry shed, thinking that they couldn't possibly have arrived home yet. There they were; all fast asleep on their perches. All except one, who muttered sleepily: "Uk-uk."

It is edifying to note the general taste in music. Although few of the animals are greatly moved by Beethoven, Bach or Mozart, they make up for this possible defect by tense appreciation of Strauss, Gilbert and Sullivan, Chopin when brilliantly rendered by a first-rate pianist, and some opera music *without* the singers. Opening marches are greatly in favour.

But, could the greatest opera singers in the world be assembled at Pant Glas, I fear they would meet with a cool reception if in full voice.

Snip has only to hear a singer, to wince. The horses and goats show great enthusiasm at many an introduction, which for them is entirely ruined when interrupted by the human voice.

It gives me some satisfaction to state that pop music offends their euphonic senses even more than singers do.

On Party evenings doors have to remain closed because Gazelle and Jane are apt to recall their youth. I don't mind one huge goat or the sheep retiring to their once favourite sofa or armchair, but they bring friends in with them. Flowers are whipped out of vases and wall-brackets; cigarettes are swallowed complete with tin foil and packet.

I admit that there have been embarrassing moments on such evenings. These only happen when we have a human guest who likes animals—in their place. It isn't long before seclusion of the sitting-room is sought, where my mother is offered commiseration for having a daughter with such odd tastes.

On one occasion the visitor, who adored—simply *adored*—animals, had decided to prolong her visit by another week because of superb weather. There was nothing to see outside except animals, so she decided to knit by a log fire. That room had more wall space and no picture window.

Reluctantly I tore myself away from the terrace to take in light refreshments. Placing biscuits and cake on a side table, I didn't notice that the door was not latched.

"I was just saying to your mother, dear, that you seem to have far too much to do. What a pity you left the gate open! I suppose you can't get those dreadful creatures out now?"

I explained that I had let them in purposely, adding: "You see, it's a full moon tonight."

I received one of those anxious, searching glances before the knitting was resumed. I was glad they both faced the fire, so my spreading smile wouldn't be encouraged by my mother or noticed by our guest.

I made coffee and took it in to them, halting in the doorway before bursting into laughter.

How quiet Niall can be when she tip-toes in to plunder! They were all twelve wickedly silent as they devoured cake, biscuits and a large ball of knitting wool. That last was in Bambi's mouth and subsequently rescued. Knowing that the raid was discovered, she bucked round the room, stretching the wool round furniture as she went.

The dogs, who had followed me into the house, had been left in the other room because of our animal-adorer. Jane, who had hesitated in the doorway, suddenly realized that no dogs were present, so landed four-square on her sofa beside the outraged adorer.

"Mer!"

Had Jane's usual and polite greeting been replied to in level terms, or even ignored, pandemonium would have been averted. But a horrified exclamation, followed by: "Shoo! Shoo! Oh, you beastly things. Now see what they've done!" wasn't helpful.

It took me some minutes to return my satanic ones to the terrace before restoring order in the room and apologizing for the borrowed wool, which miraculously wasn't broken.

There is nothing as painful as laughter when it has to be subdued. For I kept seeing Jane's bland expression as, with neatly lowered head, she charged. Why not? She had been "shooed", and had no intention of staying where she wasn't wanted.

"Mer!"

Unfortunately her head attack coincided with the moment when the visitor bent down to regain her precious ball of wool. She ended up on the sofa, head first, while Jane toddled out with quiet dignity, repeating:

"Mer!"

Outside the revellers continue to amuse themselves, and me. Long after the moon has made the subtle change from evening to night, by deepening her shade to gold, they saunter, twirl, doze, nibble, or lean against the yellow doors of the cottage, according to mood.

Belle, five goats and Michael have been greatly impressed by Grieg's *Cowkeeper's Tune and Country Dance*. With heads twisted round in approval, there has been a decided pastoral swing to their haunches. Others prefer more forceful music. All are content, with or without it.

From the writing-room, to which I have retired to work, the natural sounds are melody enough: owls hooting in the forest, the satisfying crunch of teeth on grass or an occasional clash of horns, as moon-crazed goats toast their ineffable happiness. And always, always the laughter of the brook below.

"Mmmmmmmmm!"

It is Bess who, standing in the gateway, calls back to Siriol. It could well mean: "Come dear, I'm leaving." He follows obediently. Moments later Belle crashes after them. Then in single file the three walk sedately down the stone path through the woods to the lower fields, where they will spend the rest of the night.

Suddenly I know that the precincts are empty. The goats, the sheep, the cats, kittens and dogs are sleeping wherever they choose to be.

Only owls are wakeful in silver trees. The pale blue earth is good to look upon, with its indigo hollows and guardian hills.

Ahead the sea quivers as the first moon rays touch its innocence. Long before it is arrayed in gold I, like the animals, shall sleep—*sleep*.

Chapter Twelve

IT is as difficult to choose a tense when writing of Pant Glas dwellers as it would be for a slow-flowing brook. There is infinitesimal but constant change. Each year new members of the family arrive and a few leave for carefully chosen homes. Death has little custom here.

As the goats are of particularly long lactation periods there is no need for them to reproduce more frequently than every third year.

Jane was well into her second year before she was mated. Because she is so square she kept her secret well and long.

Chita's prolific ways take serial form. So one moment I am talking of Pinto, the seal-point kitten, and the next of Lissa, the silver-grey tabby, with a four-month gap between their ages and, of necessity two gaps in my heart. But, knowing those kittens are loved by their owners, memory of them as special personalities is all gain.

Lissa, with her symmetrical black markings which make her a most attractive tabby, has her mother's sapphire eyes. Much eastern mysticism lies in them. I kept her back and back, as the litter gradually dispersed. She is so warmly affectionate and dainty; a natural consoler.

So when the call for help arrived, I swallowed and said: "Then you'd better have Lissa."

One of Chita's first sons, a handsome seal-point named

Kinkle, had lost his constant companion and brother through a swift but fatal accident. Kinkle was demented with grief.

I drove Lissa to her new family, wearing her on my shoulder as usual. She was welcomed into a luxurious home and was most intrigued by everyone.

One of Bracken's sons also lives there. Simon is a golden retriever and fit for any show bench, but he has a happier life than that! He loved Lissa from the moment they met, and as she loves everyone all was well.

Owners, children and servants met with her instant approval. Then—in came the bereaved Kinkle, better looking than ever.

"Ger-row!" he spat.

"Whoo—mee?" she purred.

"Ger-row!"

It seemed a shattering impasse but, knowing Lissa, not insurmountable. I suggested that we should leave her to settle down with whom she would and that, in time, Kinkle would be soothed by her charms.

A telephone call the next day assured me that Lissa was greatly loved by all—except Kinkle. He continued to spit and growl whenever he saw her. Knowing the depth of magic in Lissa's eyes, I said: "Leave them. He'll come round."

Sure enough two days later the message arrived. Kinkle had spent the night and much of the following day being washed and washed by her. She had washed his grief away and supplanted it with maternal care. So they are likely to live happily ever after.

The solution was a good one for all concerned, for no other friends or circumstances would have lured Lissa from me.

It is surprising how, in a large family like this, one personality here and there stands out. A cat of cats, a dog of dogs, a horse of all horses or a goat of goats. What make them so?

I suspect that there is an element of mutual attraction, for we humans are easily flattered. But there is also some extra quality, ingrained into certain animals which gives them distinction and makes them behave differently from others of their kind.

Timothy Woo, the crooked cat, was outstanding in this respect. We read each other's minds with uncanny accuracy.

Ballygiblin, the great hunter, had only to feel my lightest touch to know just what was wanted of him. How often he more than fulfilled all expectations!

Pewter, with all his aplomb, naturally lords it over any other cock, not to mention all hens. And yet, when I look at the poultry I at once see Fanny, so persistently peck-pecking in his wake. Her rather scruffy feathers offer no reason for singling her out—the artful little madam!

"Mer!" Jane will always be unique, possibly because she has had to pit her brains against so many different species, while retaining the essence of her own personality. She began as a sheep, she is a sheep and always will be. But *what* a sheep!

It is a cat's prerogative to be individual so, in mentioning Timothy Woo and Lissa, I don't minimize the charms and capabilities of Michael, China, the regal Chita and her enemy, Panda.

The dogs I see more as a group, only because I dare not single one out as being more remarkable than the others. Nada, with her steadfast gaze, is very precious. But so is Bracken, who so often slips a paw into my hand. I squeeze it, telling her that, of course, she's the best. I say the same to them all in turn. Sheena, so easy to train and dutiful, stares up at me for approval.

As for Snip, whose obedience was non-existent for the first four years of her life and who has caused me more anxiety than all the retrievers put together, she wags her stumpy tail furiously as she gazes up. She doesn't mind who is my favourite. I'm hers, and that's that.

The gentle Bess, the comedian Siriol, the lodger Belle Jones whose enjoyment of everything is so wholesome, are too individual to compare. Like Susie Hubbard, Belle has two homes where she is loved.

Who brought them all here in the first place? "How did you all get here, eh? It's got to stop, you know. We shall be ruined."

"Tee-hee-hee."

"Yes, Niall, I'd forgotten about you. Well, all kids must be firmly put down—or sold at eight weeks. I can't help it if they're tied to an iron railing in a back yard. They must go—somewhere."

"Mer!"

"It will be splendid, Jane—with mint sauce. We shall just have to steel ourselves, that's all."

"Ell-low!"

"Don't interrupt, Chita. I'm thinking."

"Mee-tew? Perr-ooo!"

"Not you, Panda dear. You do no harm up there. You can come down now. Chita's gone."

"One fine day I'll see you . . . Brrrh—snuck!"

"One fine day, Belle, you'll have to go home. Bess is in foal and you might be a bit too enthusiastic."

"Wherk-uk-uk-uk."

"That's just it, Henrietta. I must *wherk*. I've wasted all this time writing about you people. Yes, I do appreciate the eggs, dear. You know I do. But we just can't live by eggs alone."

"Mair-uh-maair!"

"Nor by bread, Bambi. Here you are; in my pocket. A cigarette for you, Belinda? Do t jostle, Niall. I'll blow it up all nostrils in turn. Wait!"

I turn on the radio. *Music while you* . . . "Wherk!" They are playing *The Teddy Bears' Picnic*:

"Ta-rum-te-dum-ta-diddly-dum . . .

Don't go down to the woods today . . ."

Deep barks encourage me into the woods. The pack must be exercised. I take many problems with me and lose them there.

It is nearly spring. A cold wind stretches the leafless trees, but the undergrowth is warm with laughing secrets. A flight of wild geese has charmed an azure sky with two silver formations, each of twenty immigrants—from Iceland?

Already the ants have opened their escape hatches to probe an uncertain world. As the sun strengthens its rays their amazing shelter stirs and heaves with the teeming life below. Strangely, the dogs never tread on that mound or on others like it, even in winter. I am glad it is so, because of the many enjoyable hours spent in watching the astonishing wares plied back and forth by arduous workers.

Eggs are carried across the mound. Sticks, some nearly a

quarter of an inch long, are rushed hither and thither as the ants sort out their rehabilitation problems.

I know that it is to be a busy spring for me. In a few weeks the goats will kid, Jane will lamb, and Chita, of course, will be at it again.

Sheena must be mated. She has run on in her single state for longer than I like. One of the best dogs in the country awaits her—one hundred and twenty miles away! What should I do without Belle Jones and Susie Hubbard on such occasions? Their owners fall to at once and most ably mind the family. Bless them!

Presently I, like the ants, shall have rehabilitation problems. Not yet—why worry? Not yet, not yet.

The very next morning, a cold and blustery one, I go out as usual to feed and milk.

"Mmmmmmmm!"

"Where are the others, Bess?"

Siriol soon tells me where he is. Belle has gone to her other home, for honest work with timber carrying.

Two cocks, who have been hailing the morn for the better part of an hour, strut out with their hens to gobble corn.

The goats? That's strange. Where is the usual scuffle for feeding bowls? Where are the scufflers? Thinking that the goat train must have left early, I have just decided to leave the bowls in the bin, when a head pops round the corner.

"Hello, Malpas. Have you missed the train?"

The billy-goat is silent but looks interested in the bin. So I place a solitary bowl, which he usually has to share with another, before him. It's his due, but I am not to know that— yet.

Sauntering past the first stable I stop in amazement. The goats are there, just thinking of coming out to look for me. Niall blocks the doorway and cries: "Hee-hee-hee!"

I rush back for their breakfast, wondering at their odd behaviour, before it occurs to me to take a roll call. All there —except . . . There is no brown goat present. "Belinda!"

No reply. By this time Bess has joined me, leaving a handful of unfinished food in her bucket. That in itself is extraordinary; no less is her behaviour as she pushes past me to go into the second stable.

She sings softly: "Um-mmm-um-mmmm!" And then I know.

There, in the far corner of the stable, is a very much pre-occupied Belinda. At last she looks up and cries: "Maair!"

"Belinda—you clever, clever girl!"

She stands over me, while I drop to my knees, exclaiming: "Oh, how—*beautiful!*" She noses me gently. Bess, satisfied that the new twins are in safe keeping, chortles as she goes out.

I choke back disappointment as I discover that the perfect Anglo-Nubian replica of Belinda, even to the drooping ears, is a billy.

Warm beneath him, dry and shining, is a clump of gold. As I stretch out my hand it rises to an astonishing height, yawns, stretches and walks quite steadily into my lap. Supposing it's another boy?

A moment later I hug her thankfully. "But, my darling, you're pure *gold*—Goldus!"

She is still that colour and will be. Her eyes are pale blue and she behaves differently from the other kids. Goldus comes at call, jumping into my arms. She smothers me with kisses then follows me like a dog.

There is no special reason for this behaviour. I had no time to single her out because the subsequent days were too busy welcoming new kids.

The following morning Niall was missing. I found her in the barn with triplets. As she had kept the herd from Belinda at the crucial time, so she had segregated herself. She had one brown daughter; the other two were sons.

On the same day more goat triplets were born. The local vet was patient, for sons were mingled with daughters and born hours and days apart. He thinks of getting a helicopter!

Bambi's daughter, Harmony, has music written all over her; staves, minims, crochets and, on each foreleg, two black chords. She is of Chita's colouring, but there the likeness to a Siamese cat ends. When the two get together I guess that the tempo will be *presto*!

Now in a box near the fire Chita purrs like an engine to four white kittens. A week ago the dogs paid homage. They sit patiently in a row, heads on one side, entranced to see eight tiny sapphires peeping through widening slits.

A golden hen is sitting on thirteen eggs. From her cosy box she waits for the miracle with unblinking eyes. Only ten days from now! I feel a thrill of excitement at the prospect of seeing yellow chickens again.

It's ridiculous, I know, to experience such eager joy as each new member of the family arrives. At times I make feeble attempts to justify their existence to inquirers.

A car is arriving. A friend leaps out.

"My dear, I was so afraid you'd be writing. It's such ages. I felt I had to call on such a day."

It is a lovely day. I show her the new stock.

"They're quite adorable—now. But what are you going to do with them?"

"Nothing."

"But you've lashings of milk already. I know you feed the other animals with it, but you don't want all *these*."

"Kids don't give milk." I explain that it will be two years before they are productive.

"But my *dear*, you'll never do any writing. How's it going?"

"I'm not writing a novel at present."

"I shouldn't think so with all these to look after."

"They really look after themselves."

"But what *use* are they?"

"They're happy. Come and have coffee."

"Ell-ow!"

"Not kittens again? You'll never sell this lot."

"Indeed I shall. I've a waiting list. But I might keep one daughter."

"Really! You're hopeless. You *don't* let the cat drink out of the milk jug?"

"No, not really." Absent-mindedly I pass her Chita instead of the milk jug.

"Ger-row."

"Oh look—look! There's a new goat train."

"A—*what*?" she asks.

I don't stay to explain. Through the trees I have just seen the four kids shunting uphill, led by Goldus. She turns left; they follow. She turns right; so do they. She jumps the brook and

187

so do two more. One hesitates on the far side, bleating. Goldus returns for her and, with a sharp head action, butts her over.

So—it will be *Goldus*. I have glimpsed Niall, staring from a field away in silent approval. Solemnly she advances towards the kids. Her manner to her own child is surprising. She nips her rump, then shoves her into line behind Goldus. Then she stands, watching, as Goldus shunts off again. It's not long before the four are leaping and dodging, scrambling, darting, skipping, until Goldus lies down in the sun. The other three do so instantly beside her.

Niall wanders over to me. "Mair-er-aair."

"I think your choice is right, Niall. But not yet—not yet, old lady?"

"Mair."

Having pressed her head against me, she wanders slowly into the Dovey field, finds Bambi who is nibbling blackthorn and brings her back at a good pace to where the kids are sleeping.

Then, without a sound, Niall walks away towards the path to the lower fields. She is still in sight when the entire herd appears from nowhere to fall in step behind her. All except Bambi, whose turn it is to mind the young.

I hurry back to my guest, with apologies.

"Is anything wrong? You went tearing out in such a hurry?"

"Nothing's wrong. I've made a wonderful discovery."

"What's that?"

"I've just found—the heroine for my next book."

A tentative look precedes the remark: "I know all writers are quaint. Perhaps if you went out more? Well, there it is. I must go now."

" *Must* you?"

"Come and see me soon. I think you should. Of course, it's very lovely here, but nothing ever *happens*, does it?"

"Sometimes. It was nice of you to come."

"Er-reow!" Michael springs off the visitor's car, lashing his tail. He runs forward a few steps before calling back: "Er-reow."

I am torn between speeding the parting guest and hurrying after the tabby cat. He seems to be on one of his missions.

At last I am able to follow him anxiously. The kids are safely in Bambi's care, so it can't be that. He lures me to the oak woods, then doubles back to the far end of the knoll. I suspect he is taking such a course because he doesn't want anyone to follow us.

He stops at last, leaving me to look beyond him up the rising slope.

"Mer!"

"Jane!"

Beside her, on a mossy slope, is the whitest of white lambs. Jane doesn't mind my interfering; she seems to like it.

"A *daughter*, Jane. How perfectly wonderful! We'll keep her for ever and ever."

"Mer!"

With the tiny one protesting in my lap, I add: "Do you know, Jane, I ought to be where things *happen*. Not here at all."

"Mer!"

"I think so, too—plenty."

"Mmmmmmmmm!"

Bess, standing in the field below, gazes up at us. As she

turns away I follow her wise example, leaving Jane to dote on her—flock.

I watch Bess's measured tread. She is large and shines like black glass. Siriol prances up to her but, with dreamy eyes, she sees beyond him. To gain her attention he cavorts in a wide circle, bringing nose to chest as if some ghostly rider prevented him from breaking into a wild gallop. At the gentlest pace he draws in beside her, inclining his head so that their nostrils touch.

The sound she makes is less than the smallest wave breaking at ebb tide; she is saving full voice to call her child to safety when it is born.

But Siriol notes it well. Whatever the message, it sends him crazy with happiness. Taking care to move well out of range, he flings out his hind legs, bucks and is off. Round the fields he gallops, mane and tail flowing, bearing the good news. He comes back to her at a controlled gait, still trembling with excitement.

Bess nudges him back to sanity and they sink to the grass, there to lie and think into the wondrous smell of it all.

I decide to go for a stroll, alone. Well, almost alone. Nada has the most pleading eyes when I make such a simple decision.

"Very well, you come too, old lady. Just the pair of us."

But we are not quite quick enough. The other three bound after us. I forget why I decided to go alone, but it doesn't matter. A handful of dogs won't stop me from enjoying a brilliant sunset.

Already cyclamen is weaving across saffron clouds to tease the far mountains with uncanny light. From the top of the knoll patchwork fields lie under a band of turquoise. The sea is grey.

The horses, who now graze side by side, are in a crimson field edged with olive green. And a pale light, like morning, creeps in from the north.

From that point, or from any other rise, there is so much to see that it's some time before I am aware of being followed. It is a gentle awareness, brought alive by the snapping of a twig followed by: "Uk-uk." No wonder the poultry are late going to bed on such an evening.

I turn round to see—that I am not alone. Nose to tail, beak to stern and in single file, quite seriously, almost the entire family is wending after me.

Three dogs dart back to my heels. Not Snip; she's too cautious because Niall, with her train, is just behind me. And next to Niall is Goldus, the golden kid. Because I bend down to speak to her, she jumps on my knee before leaping back to teach the other kids advanced acrobatics.

To prevent congestion I saunter up and down, through the oak woods, across open fields to the one which offers the widest view of sea, estuary and mountains.

China, white tail erect, races ahead to meet Michael who waits for us in a hedgerow. Possibly the one cat explains to the other that Chita is too busy to wend because of her kittens.

The horses amble towards us, grazing as they move over the brow.

They are all there, idling in groups or singly. I have no need to be aware of them because they are happy. So I can gaze at the sea which is now deep pink.

Colours are racing in fabulous disorder towards the ball of flame beyond Bardsey Island. All blues, yellow and vivid shades are losing strength to the ultimate glory in the west.

And cool, beneath the gorgeous canopy, in undulating shape and utter peace is Pant Glas; the green valley—the valley of animals.